KISSING THE ORANGE

A NOVEL

JONATHAN O'BRIEN

Copyright © Jonathan O'Brien, 1995.
All rights reserved.

The moral right of the author has been asserted.

All characters in this publication are fictitious, and any references to real persons, living or dead, are purely coincidental.

This book is sold subject to the condition that it shall not, by way of trade or otherwise, be lent, re-sold, hired out, or otherwise circulated without the publisher's prior consent in any form of binding or cover other than that in which it is published and without a similar condition including this condition being imposed on the subsequent purchase.

Distributed by Brookside Publishing
Dundrum, Dublin.

Cover Design by Portfolio.

Published by Horseshoe Books.

TO THÉRÈSE

SUMMER	....	PAGE 6
AUTUMN	....	PAGE 133
SPRING	....	PAGE 157
WINTER	....	PAGE 166

The gramophone plays, exists, everything turns. The gramophone exists, the heart beats: turn, turn liqueurs of life, turn jellies, syrups of my flesh, sweetnesses . . . The gramophone . . .

NAUSEA JEAN-PAUL SARTRE

> '*Why won't you buy me a ring, an emerald, a diamond, anything?*'
> '*It's a tradition, a rule, I hate rules.*'
> '*Why don't you grow up . . . you're just like a child ... I want a ring, a decent ring and you're trying to get out of it.*'

* * *

The sun came out, vivid, simple and clear, bathing the island in a silver glow, a light that ran its fingers over the dark struggle of the Atlantic sea, and broke across the suburbs of Dublin into the muslin drapes of that house.

A trickle of saliva ran between her breasts. Apricot lips with dark waved hair that bounced around her shoulders as she rode him hard. She built up an easy rolling momentum, over and over the bed creaked like a metronome. Her nipples taut, swollen hard, the soft touch of his hands forcing tiny drops of milk. She breathed in a line of quick gasps. Her basque rode up, pushing the swell of her breasts even higher. His hands moved through her suspenders, pulling her towards him. She shuddered right through, up to a higher place, driving till the shaft became hers to control and use beyond him for her own pleasure, riding, using it, possessing it. She slid across it, withdrawing, mounting, rejoicing until the sensation inside her became the swell of her clitoris and the expectancy of her release. Her outstretched hands splayed in the light. Her breasts filled out as her orgasm waved up and she ground down moaning. The place that she wanted she began to find. He grabbed her hair, pulled her head down and covered her lips with his mouth. Her spring uncoiled as she let out her moan, and his fingers sank deep into the flesh of her ass. The door of the bedroom swung open.

* * *

She pulled the blankets over herself. He looked at the door, their son Michael, seven, stood with a lighted match in his hand.

'Look Daddy!' he exclaimed. 'Look I got it to light just like you.'

'Where did you get that? God Almighty, a match a fuckin' match.'

But the little boy remained fascinated by the flame licking around the wood.

'Look it's burning, it's smoking, Daddy.'

Brian shot up, pointing at his son.

'You blow that out, you hear me, blow it out now, Jesus Mary and Joseph, have you no common sense? How many times have I told you, Christ Almighty, you'll burn the house down. Ciara did you see that?'

The flame burnt against the boy's little finger.

'Ow!' he cried.

The boy looked at him.

'We can buy another one.' he said.

'For God's sake, all the money I have is invested in this place.'

'No it isn't,' the boy said.' Mummy has loads of pennies. They're in the kitchen, I saw them in a bottle!'

'Come here,' Brian said laughing at him 'and give me a kiss.'

'I'll give you a big kiss,' the boy said, moving to him.

'And I'll give Mummy a big kiss too.'

He thought that nothing could be better than the pleasure of children and the picture of happiness on his wife's face. He looked at the corners of her lips and saw the crease of a smile curl into the biggest grin.

Together with life.

* * *

White clouds reflected cold light, a light that cut through the rain, casting a shadowless leaden aura.

A coffin sat solid on its trolley, mahogany covering the shroud of death's mask. Mass-cards on top, some open, the remainder in their envelopes. The Church of Our Lady of the Wayside with its wooden pews engraved at each end. The imposing ornate tabernacle. The stone altar embellished with flowers and candles. Saint Peter. Our Lady of Fatima. Saint Louis. The Sacred Heart of Jesus. The four chapels. The smell of incense.

Jenny wore black and stood erect, her mother on one side, her younger sister Rachel with her tears, on the other. The pain of it all etched across her face and St. John the Baptist touching her with a sliver of light. The deepest sorrow and sense of loss, that only comes with the finality of death, flooded over her. She went back to Portrush and to Portstewart, the picnics, the camogie matches, the animals. The way he used to sing to her when she was a baby.

'Oh Daddy, I love you so much, why do you have to go now?'

'In nomine patris et filius et spiritus sanctus. Amen.'

She thought about how earlier in the mortuary she had touched him without the magic of life in his skin, feeling his forehead and how she had let a desperate moaning cry out of her that she never knew existed. A grief she couldn't understand.

The priest approached and held her mother's hands, he came over to her, so near that she smelt the oil in his hair and felt the ruffle of silk robes. She thought back on the divorce and the great way her father had carried it and the time her mother screamed at him in that restaurant in Belfast and the way he had turned before he left them and said to her, 'I'll always love ye Jenny, no matter what happens between yer mother and myself.'

Mourners shuffled to the front of the church and because of the glare in her eyes, she was unsure.

They lined up in front of her.
'Sorry for yer troubles.'
'Sorry for yer troubles.'
'He was a good man.'
'God bless ye all.'
'Jenny, I knew yer father well.'
'Sorry for yer troubles.'
'Thanks for coming.' she whispered.
'Thank yeu for comin'.'
'Yer very good.'
'Thank yeu for comin'.'

Her best friend Valerie held her and they both let go, the fierce uncontrollable sobbing rang out through the crypt of memory.

There were landowners from Ballymena and Ballycastle, farmers from Garvagh, all his customers.

There were the blood-lines and love and respect. She tried to be strong, dignified, not to let go again. In her mind her father's words:

'Ye'll be alright Jenny, ye don't worry, watch that temper of yers and ye'll be fine ... jus' fine.'

Two men in suits wheeled the coffin out of the church past the visitor's book, from the balcony the organist played *'Ave Maria'*. Her uncles lifted the coffin and carried it on their shoulders into the rain and through the town of Kilrea, past the empty pubs, the lifeless supermarket, his abandoned surgery, past the great emptiness created by years of migration. When the procession reached the entrance of the cemetery, her eyes gazed across the rows of tombstones until they rested on the piper. The blowing murmurs of the pipes whined through the drizzle and at the graveside the priest said the rosary.

She watched his lips mouthing the prayer and looked into her mother's face to see if there was anything, even some small indication of respect, to witness her uttering the prayer even once but she saw only silence and indifference. The lines on her mother's brow, furrowed by the bitterness of self-control, betraying years of emotional isolation and knotted anguish. The priest blessed the mahogany coffin with holy water.

She looked back across the graveyard, past the tombstones, past the history of the dead of this Northern community, back to the piper who played 'Kiss me my sweet', her father's favourite melody. The one that he had sung through her life.

The synthetic grass was pulled away and four wooden planks which had supported it were stacked up. The coffin was lowered with running ropes into earth.

She felt then that he was watching her, speaking words of life, telling her that he would always be alive in her, and in the children that she would have. She took comfort from the hope of his silent message.

She had a strange feeling about a passion that would take her away from his death mask.

A warm tear trickled across her cheek and splashed against a blade of grass.

Her mother stood on it.

Alone with Death.

Jonathan O'Brien

SUMMER

May, 1992. Late evening in Tallaght. Last of the bird song and fading light. Boys played football in a field, bicycles and kit-bags lay behind the goal posts. Girls on a wall chewing gum, smoking, watching the game and nudging each other. A Cortina and a rust-eaten Datsun parked together at the back of a shopping centre. A refuse tip leaned against the wall, out of it dripped plastic bin-liners.

Light shone from under the steel door of the shop unit and smoke billowed out of an aluminium chimney. The door opened, a man in a white apron appeared, flicking a cigarette butt into the yard. He went back in and left the door ajar.

Inside the bakery two men in white coats covered in spits of dough, lifted a metal bowl onto mixer arms. One of them portioned measures of whole-grain flour onto a weighing scales.

Heat burnt out sweat from white skin.

In one corner, boxes of raisins and margarine, bags of flour, sugar and bran, in the other, cartons of liquid egg and churns of buttermilk.

The baker walked to the sink and attached a garden hose to a tap, he carried it to the mixing bowl and turned on the water as Brian walked in from the store room.

'Put your cap back on, I don't want the Eastern Health Board on my back.' Brian roared.

There was no reaction.

'I said put your fuckin' cap on!'

'Yeah, yeah I heard you.'

'You showed in late last night, we start at ten.'

'Yeah I said I heard ye.'

He walked up to him. 'Who the fuck do you think you're talkin' to? Where the fuck do you think you are? Jesus Christ do you think I'm running the business for charity, for fuck's sake don't you fuckin' talk back to me like that. Every night I get the same shit from you, every fuckin' night you're talkin' back to me, now put your fuckin' cap on.' He grabbed the cloth cap from the table and threw it at the baker. The man replaced it on the table and Brian exploded.

'What do you think you're doing, Jesus Christ, right get the fuck out of here, get your gear and fuck off, you're out, fired, history, over, fired, fuck off.'

'I want me money.'

His partner Frank standing by the oven intervened:

'Come back on Friday, we'll sort it.'

The baker removed his overalls and walked out, his eyes all over Brian who had gone to the oven to read the thermostat.

'This oven's too slow. Frank! Have you got the order?'

'Yeah, 120 dozen.'

Brian read from a clipboard.

'Right, 120 dozen donuts, 60 dozen scones, 100 Browns.' He called over to one of the bakers, asking, 'Have you done the mixes yet?'

'Yeah, yeah I've got them.'

He looked hard at the sheet and wiped his forehead.

'Who's the first driver?'

'Willie, he's Northside.' Frank replied.

'We'll never get it out, what time?'

'5.30. around there.'

'Jesus, we'll never do it, c'mon lads.'

The fierce war continued with each person in it knowing his own responsibility. No one encroached, each one knew his duty and each soldier carried his weapon. A good team. And a million heads slept quietly outside.

'What's that noise?' he asked, staring at the oven.

'Shit, it's the oven, the thermostat, it's going down.'

Frank said, 'Jesus not again, I'll never get to bed, open the door will you, let the heat out, Brian get the door open.'

He pulled the lever on the outside of the door, hot smoke billowed out filling the bakery in a fog of white heat.

'Get me a screwdriver quick!' Frank demanded, and unhinged the casing by the door. Inside there were rows of fuses and heavy gauge wires. It was a revent convection oven, eight foot in height, and at least twenty years old. They'd borrowed two thousand to buy it and hauled it across Ireland on the back of a rented lorry.

'The Sparks, his number's on the wall, beside the phone', Frank said. 'Tell him I need three phase cable, half metre, and to bring some fuses, we'll never get the orders out, tell him to get over here fast, who's the second driver?'

At four o'clock the donut machines were switched on and the oil burnt up to 270 degrees. The hoppers were filled with mix and the white sludge dropped in round circles onto steel plates. Perfect ring donuts were created and finally fell into basins of sugar and the floor started to slip.

Brian was tired.

He wanted to go home.

* * *

He drove his Peugeot Estate through the calm Dublin morning, his window open as he listened to the clacking sound of seagulls wheeling and diving above the red towered buildings at St. Nicholas Place. By the quays a new building boom had started, it was here that Dublin's Viking history had been ripped out by developers and huge cranes balanced like inverted crutches against the skyline.

He passed by the Brazen Head, down Bridge Street Lower, going across the Liffey and looked up to the turquoise-green copper roof of the Four Courts. The rock of Irish law curling beside its eternal bed-mate, the tired stenching Liffey that swelled towards Dublin Bay. He passed across Church Street Bridge, waited for the traffic lights to change, watching the seagulls on the walls, their white droppings trailing to the water. He stared at a tramp going through a litter bin with intent and the balconies of flats with washed underwear, blouses and shirts hanging out on clotheslines. He listened to the news of the North and the troubles, bored he switched it off and drove on to his house in Swords.

They lived in a quiet cul-de-sac and he pulled into the

driveway in front of his box and switched off the engine. As he put the key into the front door, he heard the telephone ring. He walked in and picked it up.

'No I haven't forgotten the bank, at what time, yeah 3 o'clock, I'll do it myself, will you get the Cash and Carry? Okay, see you later.'

He put the phone back. Everything was silent. His children asleep, she was asleep. In the kitchen he made tea and sat down, his forehead in his hands. He stroked his face and as exhaustion set in, his head tilted over onto his arms. He slept at the table. Some business.

* * *

'I'm going to buy you flowers.'
'I don't want flowers.'
'Every woman wants flowers.'
'I'm not every woman, I want a ring ... I want you.'
'Listen, I'm buying you flowers and that's it.'

*

'Brian, you're tossing and turning.'
'I can't sleep.'
'Can't you say the rosary or something?'
'The rosary!'
'Yes, you know Hail Mary ...'

*

'You know Ciara, when I make some money, I'll get a big place, somewhere I can have a piss in my own garden without being looked at.'
'Brian, I don't want a big place, I only want your time and a ring, I never seem to see you.'

*

'You've cut yourself shaving, are you alright, darling? Listen, don't go today, you're all uptight, look at the other side of your chin, you're cut to pieces, stay here with me, lie down. I'll make some tea. Forget the bakery, come back to bed and put your head down.'

*

'Brian, I feel really horny, I need more sex.'
'I'm knackered.'
'Well I need more, last night wasn't enough, you were too quick and I haven't come in ages.'

*

'Brian, I hope you know that I'm a very attractive lady.'
'Yeah, I know.'
'Well, today, I was chatted up in the supermarket and yesterday in the bank, so pay more attention to me and less to that business.'

*

'Today I'm going to make lettuce soup, cook a leg of lamb and I'm going to make chocolate pudding with brandy and you are staying home.'
'I think you only want to fatten me up so that no one else will look at me.'
'Darling, I cook for you 'cos I love you.'

*

They're in a jeweller's shop.
'I love those earrings.'
He buys them and says:

'Don't mention the ring.'
'Why not?'
'Okay, let's go, c'mon, out, now!'

*

'Sometimes I don't know how I ended up with you.'
'Well you did, tough shit.' he says.
'Sometimes I wish you had a profession, gone to college instead of that filthy business.'
'What's wrong with the bakery, it's a living, isn't it?'
'Ever since we've been married we've been broke, always trying to make ends meet, I'm sick of it, I hate it and I never see you and when I do, you smell of burnt fat.'

*

They watch a film on T.V.
'Brian, you wouldn't have an affair would you?'
'Don't be mad.'
'No, would you?'
'Ciara, I am having an affair, it's called the bakery business.'

* * *

The bank manager readjusted the file in front of him. His glasses sitting on the bridge of his nose, his skin drink-marked with the red blotches of broken capillaries and the corners of his mouth crossed with the sneer of a little power.

It was a simple, stark office and the rain splashed lightly against the window panes, running down the glass in long erratic drops. He sharpened a pencil with method, brushed the waste into his palm and rubbed his hands together over the wastebin. A wire basket rested on the desk and behind it was a monitor, in front of him a blank pad of writing paper and a thin file marked 'O'Neill'.

Brian walked in. The manager stood up, put the pencil on the foolscap and extended a thin hand.

'I'm glad you could come at such short notice, Mr O'Neill.'

Brian shook his hand and drew up a seat. 'Would you like some coffee, Mr O'Neill?' he asked.

'Yeah, coffee, thanks, coffee, thanks very much.' Brian answered, surprised.

Two minutes later the man returned with a cup and saucer, a biscuit balanced on the side. He sat down and watched Brian drinking the warm coffee.

'I'm looking after your account from here on in,' he started. 'I've just come in from Head Office. I'm under audit. Your account has come up for review and we think, I mean I think, I mean, I mean that, well, I mean that you're showing all the signs of overtrading.'

Brian had been distracted by the rain's patterns on the window. He turned his head.

'Oh yes, I have our accounts ready, I can give you a full set.'

'I'm sorry Mr O'Neill, put very simply we can't renew your existing facility. That is what I mean and what I'm telling you here is that your present facility is being withdrawn.'

He bent forward and pulled a pencil out from a tin and began to tap it on the desk, he stood up, brushed the cloth of his suit, straightened his tie and ran his finger inside the lapel of his jacket. He stared out at the rain.

'Mr O'Neill, this is a recession, times are hard, I don't like doing this anymore than the next man, it's not only you, there's plenty of others in the same boat. Sometimes I walk out of here and I don't know if I'm going to reach my car in one piece. You understand my position, yes?'

Brian confused and angry, opened and closed the clasp on his watch.

'Would you care for more coffee?'

Brian, stared at him, his hands clenched in hard, skin stretched out over his knuckles.

'Coffee, coffee, you want me to drink coffee, you take the rug from under me and you want me to drink coffee!'

'Mr O'Neill there's no need to raise your voice like that.'

Brian sprang up.

'Raise my voice, raise my voice, do you know what you're doing? Do you know what you are fucking doing to me?'

The manager raised his hands.

'Please Mr O'Neill, it isn't me.'

'It isn't you, it's never you is it? It's never you, it's always some cunt who's at some fuckin' meeting, isn't it?'

All fired up, with his fists tight on the table.

'I'm out there, you understand I'm out there, I'm fuckin' out there, grafting, I've never screwed a bank in my life, I've never had to borrow in my life. I need this money, I need the money to survive, I need the money now! I fuckin' need it, can't you see that?'

'Mr O'Neill you can't use language like that here.'

'Fuck you, fuck you! You've taken my existence away from me and you tell me to drink coffee and not use language. You sit here in your suit telling me you're going to cut off my legs! What did you expect?'

The door half opened and a security man entered.

'Mind your own business,' Brian shouted at him.

The security man began to wrestle with him but he swivelled around and caught him full in the stomach with his right elbow. The man groaned 'Jaysus!' and raised his right hand. Brian caught it at the elbow and said: 'Use that for blessing yourself, you couldn't hit a cow's arse with a shovel!'

'Call the police, quick, the police.' someone shouted.

He pushed the security man out of the room and jammed a chair against the door.

'Mr O'Neill, Mr O'Neill, this is not on, Mr O'Neill! Please stop getting so excited.'

'Excited, is it, excited, don't fuckin' tell me I'm excited, I'm out there working eighteen hours a day, seven days, one hundred hours a week on a measly three thousand pound overdraft, I take nothing out of my business. So don't tell me I'm excited.'

He put his hand into his jacket, pulled out a sugar covered J Cloth and wiped his face. Some sugar fell on the table, sprinkling over the blank page of foolscap.

'I have to pay wages, some of my guys have families and you bastard, you bastard, you give me fuckin' coffee, and sharpen your fuckin' pencils, who do you think you are?'

The door rattled as bank staff outside tried to force it.

Someone called out 'Are you alright Mr Davy? Mr Davy, are you okay?'

Brian, his face full of anger, ignoring the door, pointed his finger at the man's head.

'Ah, fuck this, fuck you, fuck you anyway!'

As he was about to leave he turned to face the manager:

'Don't say you're only doing your job, don't say that.'

The security man lunged at him as he came out. Brian blocked him, jumped over the swing doors and moved quickly to the exit, kicking the main door open. The man running after him, repeating, 'Hey you, you, hey you!'

People stared as he rushed out and when he was out about twenty yards, he lifted his head and roared into the rain:

'Fuuuuuuuuuuuuuuuck!'

The sound of a siren drifted over.

* * *

Frank left the Christian Brothers and studied in the College of Commerce in Rathmines. Born in Galway, he played rugby for Wanderers and travelled extensively around Europe. He retained the energetic walk of someone who could break into a sprint at any moment. He had sandy thinning hair that covered laughing eyes, the nose was flat like a boxer's.

He always wore waistcoats and when he made one of his

pronouncements, put his hands into the lip pockets before delivery. He had a taste for alcohol, good coffee and tall women.

Like Brian he was black and white in some areas and utter madness in others, but these two had different strengths and it worked. They'd met at a party when Frank expounded his theories on the opposite sex, Brian was in stitches. They became friends, threw three thousand each into the kitty and started the bakery.

All of the business was wholesale, so there was a real need to monitor invoices, to watch the cash-flow and everyone wanted sixty days, ninety days, one hundred and twenty days, it was tough as hell, it was worse than that.

The tiled floor was pristine clean. Frank, leaned back against the warm oven, his two hands in his waistcoat pockets.

'And what did he say?'

'He told me to forget it, I told you.' Brian replied, scraping at the floor with the toe of his shoe.

'Jesus, the bastard after two years, we've been paying all their charges, paying the interest, we've only gone over the limit twice, who was he? The usual guy!'

'No, he was new, trying to push the boat out, you know what I mean.'

'We'll have to get it elsewhere, we'll have to resolve this, how could he do it to us? Did you lose your head again?'

'After he said no, yeah, well I did.'

Brian grimaced.

'What did you do, c'mon Brian, what did you say to him?'

'I said what I had to say after he told me he'd withdrawn the overdraft.'

Brian shrugged his shoulders.

'How much are we owed on invoices?'

'I don't know, eight hundred, maybe nine, around that figure.'

'Christ is that all, we'll need that this week-end to survive.'

Frank picked up a sack of sugar and stacked it.

'You lost your head again, have you any idea how to work with these guys?'

Brian raised his voice.

'I don't want an argument, the simple story is we haven't got it, we can't write any more cheques. Listen, either we get cash from our existing accounts or we're out of business. I don't need a lecture'.

'Jesus, I wish you didn't have such a short fuse.'

'Listen Frank, I was the person doing the asking, believe me, it was nothing to do with my fuse.'

'Yeah, sure.'

The phone rang, he went over to answer it.

'Who? Ah yeah, Mr Ellis.' he went silent, listened and spoke.

'Are you sure? No charges! You're absolutely sure? Jesus, that's brilliant, thanks, send the bill to me here will you, at the bakery, it's only I don't want Ciara ... no ... I said, it's well that, she doesn't need to know.'

He put the phone down.

'Marital counselling from solicitors, now I've heard it all!'

'What's the story?' Frank asked.

'The trouble in the bank, they're dropping the charges, something about bad publicity, fuck them.'

Frank lifted a bag of flour over. He turned to his partner.

'This is a disaster!'

Brian walked over to the kettle and put it on. He took two mugs, put in tea bags and waited. He shook his head and looked up.

'What about retailing?' he suggested.

'Where?'

'Markets, fairs, I dunno.'

'What are you saying?'

'I'm saying, we get a load of donuts and go to Henry Street on Saturday, it's a busy street, it's always packed.'

Frank looked incredulous.

'And then?'

'We put them on trolleys and sell them.'

'Ah, you're crazy, I didn't end up getting an education to sell gear on Henry Street, how much are we talking about?'

'I don't know, six for a pound, seven, maybe eight.'

Brian sipped tea from his mug, his head down deep in thought. 'Listen, why don't we make 100 dozen this weekend and see what happens.'

'You're mad, I'm not going to Henry Street, with the traders and the prams, you're fuckin' joking!'

'Well you tell me, what do we do?'

'Listen I've a business degree, I can't be going there as a street trader, mother of God.'

He buried his head in his hands.

'No woman will go near me if I'm seen there, no, no, no way.'

Brian shrugged his shoulders.

'Well I'm into it. If someone doesn't do something we're fucked ... we lose all this!'

He swept his arm in a circle.

'Look Frank you go and get as much money in as you can from the accounts. I'm going out on Saturday morning, if it doesn't work, so be it, at least we tried.'

Frank put his cup down and smiled.

'You're fuckin' mad, you know that.'

'Frank, get some of the invoices paid, will you?'

He brought both cups over to the sink, washed them out and they left.

* * *

He parked the van behind Moore Street, beside Henry Street the real soul of the inner city with its dealers and its history. A breeze carried the scent of hops and barley over from the Guinness Brewery.

He took the trolley out, put it on the ground, took out four cases of donuts and rested them on it. He locked the van and

Kissing the Orange

made his way down Moore Street, watching traders leaning over stalls full of vegetables and fruit and listened to the fierce bantering.

A woman sold flowers stacked in tins and stuck fivers into her cleavage. Over on the right, underneath the Ilac Centre, another filleted fish, whiting, cod and sea bass slipping across timber, the entrails with the flies in a white plastic bucket at her feet. Beside her another woman sold chickens and a man in a black miner's coat stood on a horse-pulled cart loaded with boxes of onions, cauliflowers, apples and tomatoes, sacks of potatoes, carrots and cabbages. A butcher carried a pig's carcass on his shoulders, his white coat patched with blood.

Brian pushed the trolley through Moore Street.

'What are you selling Mister?'

'What's that you have in them cases?'

'What's in them boxes? Look ma, it's buns.'

'Here mister, give us some cakes, will ya? Here, how much are youse selling them for? Mister, Mister.'

He pushed the trolley out into the middle of the street, glanced up and down, three, maybe, four times and said in a low voice:

'Eight donuts in a bag for one pound.'

He looked again, nervous as hell, watching the faces and went a little louder.

'Eight donuts in a bag for a pound.'

Nothing happened.

A boy shouted 'Here mister give us a donut, give us one of them cakes'.

The traders had moved up to the top of the street, chattering and whispering like magpies. One of the women approached him, wearing a flowered apron and the smile of a happy life. She thrust a pound coin into his hand and said, 'There's your hansel, son.'

'Thanks very much, thanks.' he replied taking the luck money.

You could see he meant it.

'Youse want to go louder son, youse want to go much louder.' she advised.

He smiled and climbed up on the trolley amidst a roar of approval from the traders.

'I said eight fresh donuts in a bag for a pound.' he barked.

They all laughed, as if it was the best show in town.

'Mind the Gardaí, ya hear.'

Within moments he was surrounded by shoppers who handed him cash. He had a plastic bag over his right hand for the donuts, while with his left hand he took in the notes and coins. Shoppers were drawn to his energy.

Money, confectionery, hope everywhere, and sugar all over him; his hands, his face, his hair, his jumper.

As quick as it started, it stopped, all four cases were empty. He examined each of the boxes carefully, putting his hand into his pocket, touching the money as though he didn't quite believe what had happened.

'Go on son! Get some more, you're only startin',' they shouted.

He wheeled the trolley back into Moore Street, his head high. He put the cash out on the floor of the van and pushed all the change to one side, counting the money, each note a testament to his endeavour and enterprise. He whooped it up.

'Yes, yes, yes!'

He stuffed the money into his pocket and pulled out the remaining four crates. Again on Henry Street, he stood on the trolley but with new confidence as he cajoled the shoppers.

'C'mon get your money out of your greasy pockets, nobody but nobody can match this unbelievable price, c'mon ladies and gents, value, value, value, you'll never see it again, eight I said, yes, eight donuts in a bag for a pound, yes you madam, and you sir over there and you sir.' His hands reaching out to collect money. A trader said 'He's a natural'.

Another nodded and a shopper approached him.

'You'd say Mass.'

'I'd hear Confession,' he replied, 'but I wouldn't hear yours. C'mon, c'mon over there, and you sir, yourself madam, thank you very much.'

All the time wheeling the trolley in and out of Moore Street to avoid the Gardaí as if he'd been doing it all his life.

When he finished the second batch he took the trolley and walked back through Moore Street with Frank.

'You can do it, you can do anything you want Frank,' he said, swinging the trolley in and out of the shoppers.

'Fair dues to you, Brian boy, 150 quid in two hours, we'll make three hundred dozen next week.'

'What happens if it rains? Did you think about that?' asked Brian. 'Anyway I'm not selling three hundred dozen on my own.'

'No you're not.'

'Go on, you're not going for it!'

'All that education, and now this!' Frank smiled.

Brian looked at his partner.

'Look Frank,' he said seriously, 'the world is full of educated people who are afraid to start somewhere, but you have to do it, it's as simple as that, education means nothing. You have to put meat on the table and you've got to start somewhere.'

Frank put his arm around his shoulders.

'C'mon, I said I'm in, didn't I, let's get a pint. We'll save this business.'

'A pint for fuck's sake, champagne! Frank, champagne!'

Later as they drank, Brian had the powerful feeling of fulfilment and self-esteem knowing that at last he had become a provider to his family, his employees and himself.

* * *

May. Trinity College Dublin and it was raining. He walked through the city, passing the main entrance of the college decked in flags and bunting. Two purple cloth banners announcing the 400th anniversary celebrations flapped in the wind.

Outside the main gates a tout sold tickets and he went for it. Just like that, a whim. Ciara was delighted. She'd got good results in Trinity, studied medicine and qualified. She'd learnt about life from intense conversations in the Buttery Bar and afterwards spent three years in London as an intern, one-hundred-hour weeks and the rest of her time sleeping and having tired conversations in wine-bars and clubs in the West End. She came back to re-start in Dublin, to a future in medicine, but instead looked into his eyes in Davy Byrnes and joined her destiny to his.

It was the evening of the Ball. She was in their bedroom, sitting with her lipstick, putting the Apricot over her lips. With her red basque, red stockings and her suspenders in front of the mirror, she sucked her face in and winked at him.

'You love that colour.' he said standing at the door in his white dinner jacket.

'Apricot? I've always used it. I've always worn apricot darling, you know that.'

She laughed, stood up, walked over to the cupboard and took out a black dress. Figure-hugging, shoulders, long legs. Slipping on her shoes she bent over and started to fiddle with the buckle on the leather and again looked into the mirror, seeing the bulge in his pants she smiled big at him. The dress pinching her breasts so that the nipples crushed out. He smoked. She looked across at him.

'Can you zip me up?'

He walked to her, kissed her neck and breathed in the nectar of her sex.

'You look beautiful, better than when I first married you.'

He curled his fingers around her, smelling her hair. She looked at him and asked, 'Is the baby-sitter downstairs?'

'Yes, I let her in while you were up here.'

'We'll have to wait,' she shook her finger at him.

She walked over to a chest of drawers and pulled out a hundred necklaces, one fell onto the carpet. She picked it up and put it on. Pearls. She wasn't sure, pearls hadn't been lucky for her. She took them off and put them on again, hesitantly kissed him and went to the children's bedroom.

Their daughter, Eileen, said, 'Mummy you look lovely.'

'Thanks sweetheart, we won't be long, if Michael wakes up put him into our bed, Avril's downstairs.'

She kissed Eileen on her forehead.

'Love you darling.'

The child looked at her leaving the room.

'Have a great time Mummy.' she said, eyes open wide.

Brian entered and gave them both kisses.

'Oohh yuk, get that cigar out of here.'

He laughed at his daughter.

'Sleep tight love, snug as a bug.'

She picked it up, 'In a rug.'

Big smiles all round. When they closed the door behind them the baby-sitter got that sweet aroma of cigars, perfume and expectancy.

* * *

By evening a strong south-east wind had cut through the clouds and the rain had stopped. On the journey into town they listened to Grace Jones. She fingered her necklace, rolling the pearls between her finger and her thumb.

'You seem distant.' he said.

'I'll snap out of it.'

Her eyes turned out towards the roadside. She'd never trusted pearls.

That night it was 'Le Caprice' on St. Andrews Street with young men in black ties and girls in extravagant dresses. The Trinity young with the Trinity decadent, the Trinity intelligent with the Trinity beautiful, the Trinity hopeful with the Trinity successful.

The head waiter showed them a table. Running parallel to them, a party was in progress. Twelve, maybe fourteen, girls engaged in celebration, the table covered with the debris of the evening, happy faces enhanced with smiles of nubility, bantering and laughing as they recalled good days, one of them carrying the weight of a strong personality, held her audience with a comic tale and finished with '... he was frantic, frantic, you've never seen anything like it.' They burst into spontaneous laughter.

A piano played in the background. A limp cigarette hanging from the pianist's lips as he read the *Evening Herald*.

That night they ate tortellini with steak cooked in olive oil and they drank a soft Beaujolais that magnetised them. A tiny splash of tomato sauce speckled her chin, he lifted his napkin and dabbed it.

'You remember Davy Byrnes?' Ciara asked.

'The first time we made love?' he replied.

'God, I didn't know anything about anything, did you think it was going to be me?'

He looked at her, shaking his head, playing with his bread, rolling it around between his fingers.

'I tell you, Ciara, the first time we met I felt, well, the chemistry, I didn't know it existed until then, that instant attraction stuff.'

'You found me at the right time, I wanted children.'

'Is that it? I was only a stud!'

'Don't be ridiculous, anyway I wasn't a wallflower.'

She moved her finger along the stem of the glass.

'I wanted you, I want you now.' he said.

'Will you always want me?' she asked.

He leant over the table and kissed her. The slow kiss that told her all she needed to know.

'Go on, ye boy ye.' goaded a student from a nearby table.

They laughed, wine splashing their lips. Two flaming Sambucas were put in front of them.

One of the girls rose and stood beside the piano, letting a

great mane of red hair fall about in front of her face and sang 'Galway Bay', meeting the piano note for note, carefully breathing in with the accomplished discipline of a trained vocalist.

During the rendition, her friends at the next table played games with the men, testing weaknesses, mermaids driving the unwary to perish on rocks of temptation, each in turn glancing, a moment but enough, their eyes deep pools of enticement, their lure of Celtic sex permeating everything.

Sometime during that evening, Ciara put fingers across her forehead and flicked dark hair from it and stared across at the blonde who'd been watching her man. The one who would cause so much pain.

Later she said, 'Lets not go to the Ball'.

'Jesus, what are you on about?'

'Will you stay with me?'

'Ah, c'mon what are you saying? What's got into you?'

'I hate these pearls, I'm never wearing them again!' she said suddenly, but after a time she relented, 'Listen, why don't we try to find Mike's rooms? He's a junior Dean, he's bound to be still there.'

'He's not still lecturing?'

'Yeah he is.'

'Brilliant idea. Let's do it.'

Twelve-thirty. People left the restaurants and bars and headed for the ball. Fantasy became reality and a frenzy of merrymaking.

The Trinity Ball.

'Ladies and gentlemen. Let the party begin!'

* * *

It was the kind of clear night that told you of warm days. Outside the main gates a queue snaked past the tall iron railings, going serpentine by the railings, twisting through Nassau Street, down as far as the eye could see.

Black ties and every style of dress imaginable. Girls laughed, slugging from vodka bottles, cans of lager, throwing cigarettes, jumping the queue, waving at traffic. Two men dressed as bishops dispensed blessings to all. Further on, three girls in Victorian dress sailed past in a perfect line, all smoking. At the end of the queue, rented horse-drawn carriages mixed with cars off-loading excited cargo. Back on College Green, underneath the statue of Henry Grattan, four male students had set up a table, on top of which was placed a candelabra filled with candles flickering in the breeze, they drank port and roared their toasts.

The jostling queue maintained a steady momentum as people gained admission. Earrings splashing about faces, hats and hairnets, tight black and loose silk. Underneath the archway Ciara handed in their ticket, squeezed his hand and they walked through, passing the glass-framed notice boards into the cobblestoned square.

Once inside the College, it was a different stage. Canvas walkways were set up over the cobblestones. Girls ran about, lifting their dresses like gazelles freed from the confines of captivity. In the front Square, a man swung around the statue of George Salmon, a bottle of wine in his hand, his shirt open, his bare feet splayed out against the black stone. Below him the official photographer hustled for business. Over by the Chapel and the Dining Hall, was the Buttery Bar where men held jugs of lager and girls slipped across spilt beer.

Attracted by music, they made their way like a couple of adolescents to the stage set up behind the Buttery and danced to Prince's 'Little Red Corvette'. Afterwards they walked to the entrance of the Library where a mass of people danced barefoot to Bob Marley, their arms flailing about their bodies, some stoned, some easy with it, some dreaming, some frozen in memories of days gone by.

He saw her behind his wife, squeezed into a white dress, the blonde who'd been in the restaurant, swaying and turning with the music. The girl's face lit up as she recognised him.

Ciara dragged him away and they strolled to the Graduate's Memorial Building and climbed up three floors. When they reached the top of the wooden stairs, someone in a corridor shouted out her name and they entered a drinks party. In that room it was the clink of ice cubes, slices of lemon and tall glasses of cold white wine, crackers with stilton and water biscuits with avocado dip, ashtrays filled with cigarette butts, hardback books scattered between worn leather chairs and threadbare rugs on floor boards.

They threw themselves into the party, pumping hands and laughing about the past, renewing old acquaintances, reminiscing. There was a moment when he left Ciara, walked over to one of the windows, overlooking the cobblestones, in his eyes curiosity and intrigue as below he could see her amongst the dancers and he turned his gaze up to the distant black clouds, full of rain.

They stayed for two hours and left, mad for another dance. At the bottom of the stairs he instinctively grabbed his wife, squeezing her waist, touching her pearls, her neck, her earlobes, her hair, her breasts. Afterwards they made their way across the cobblestones to the Sports Pavilion where a band belted out its own rock and roll. He lay on the grass, her head against his chest.

The lead guitar screamed out, honest, simple and powerful, the singer deranged with his own madness, knelt over the mike, injecting everyone with his message. Out of the dawn sky, fireworks erupted into a circle of phosphorous, filling the night with pink, blue and white balls of fire. The crackle, crackle, bursting open into a great mural of exploding stars.

In the light of the fireworks, men stripped of their jackets, watched the girls, delirious, drunk and free, dancing on the grass.

In the marquees the barmen ran between kegs of lager and Guinness, girls poured drinks into pot plants, men who had come in with whiskey searched for women who hid in the arms of others. Some girls chased fun, alcohol and change for cigarettes, others threw up, opening their mouths again and again. Students pissed against walls and watched urine trickling its way around the cobblestones. Barmen cursing all of them, every tap out of drink and tills full of damp notes.

In the square under the bell tower of the campanile couples slept. In the tower itself two men rang the bell and on the grass surrounding it, people kissed and surrendered to excess, arms stretched out and lost watches, lost spectacles, lost shoes, torn dresses, lost expectations and lost virginity.

'C'mon Brian one more dance, it must be at least three, we better get back.'

'Forget time. Time doesn't matter,' he said.

'You're right. Is the big band still playing, I wonder?'

'Yeah let's go for it.' he remembered and looked up at the sky. 'I think it's going to rain.'

They scrambled off the grass and strolled through the Square, past the Reading Room, to the Exam Hall. There on stage in white jackets and red dicky bows, blowing big on brass, the St Lawrence band played 'Little Brown Jug'.

Nothing had changed. The hall was crowded and nobody knew the steps, only how to sweat themselves up. The band leader stood up, thanked everyone and announced the last number for the evening, 'Moonlight Serenade'.

They waltzed around the floor, bumping and tripping over other couples and that girl was there again, dancing with her partner as if she'd been doing it all her life. He looked over, their eyes met and his wife lifted her head to him saying, 'I'd really love to dance properly, lessons or something'.

She said 'Brian!'
She said 'Brian!'
She said 'Brian!'
He didn't hear.
The beat.
The Ball.

*   *   *

For weeks the production at the bakery and the processing and selling on Saturdays gradually created their cashflow, the excitement, temporary though it may have been, of having enough to pay bills. Frank was good at selling but slower, not taking as much but trying nonetheless and he supervised Friday nights when they baked donuts for the Saturday trade on Henry Street.

On a good week-end six or seven hundred pounds was not unusual, on a bad one three or four hundred. They employed others to sell and join in the fever, the high, coming from the feeling of beating the odds, the bankers, themselves.

Some days they were marched to Store Street Police Station and charged with illegal trading, showing up on Mondays in the District Court and receiving their punishment, a fine or a suspended sentence. The other traders told them it was nothing, nothing to worry about, that it was cheaper than paying rent.

Frank leased a two-bedroomed flat. Brian paid his debts, bought the children good clothes. The bakers and their families were fed and watered.

*   *   *

Then it rained for days. Irish rain. Hard rain that left streets pasted in great slicks of water and it was bad. Everytime you looked out of the window it was there. Covering everything with its morbid coat. Insipid veil. Even your bones ran cold with it. For six days and seven long cold nights it came down, penetrating imagination, drowning optimism, nullifying inspiration washing away all humour and good intent. It poured constantly making you feel as though there would never be another dry day. It went on and on. Dublin's pubs filled with steaming anoraks. Umbrellas left pools of water.

Smoke settled. Sounds didn't carry. People confused rain with life, with death. Irish rain, containing everything in dark embryonic water. Remorseless damp wash, and she arrived.

* * *

Brian wheeled his trolley across Henry Street, jesting with the shoppers, sugar all over him, his face, his shirt and his pants. In the break of the crowd he could see the blue caps heading towards him. Dealers with prams supporting bread-boards full of fruit, chocolates, socks, cigarettes and fruit scattered. He had ten cartons of donuts on the trolley underneath a plastic cover. In the chase one of the cartons slipped out and the entire stock cascaded. The Gardaí, embarrassed knowing the chase was over, passed him. People shook their heads, his day was done.

He started to clear them up and put them back into the cartons when he noticed the umbrella beside him.

'It's okay.' he said without looking, 'I'll manage.'

'It's such a shame.' a voice light and gentle half- uttered.

'Look it's alright.' he repeated.

He looked up to see the girl smiling at him, he heard himself inside her, kicking at the walls of her womb, a foetus desperate to be mothered.

For a moment she thought she heard a heart beat.

'Hi,' he said as though he was trying to remember.

'How ye doin'?' she asked, knowing.

'Listen, I'll do it.'

But she continued placing the cakes into the cartons. He stood up and took the plastic bags from her hand.

'No honestly it's okay, these things happen.'

'Exactly.' she said with a Northern lilt. Amused he imitated her. 'Exactly.'

She laughed, they laughed together.

* * *

He wheeled the trolley back to Moore Street, opened the door of the van and put in the crates. He walked back to the coffee shop in the Ilac Centre. She was seated by the window, letting the anticipation wrap itself around her. He bought a coffee and sat opposite her.

'How ye doin'?'

He said nothing.

'What are ye lookin' at?'

She asked stirring her spoon in her cup.

'Nothing.'

'It's a wig.' she touched her hair.

'Jesus, I'm sorry, I always put my foot in it.'

'Exactly.' she said.

'What are ye laughin' at?'

'Nothing, just the way you say that 'exactly.'

There was a pause and she put her spoon away.

'I had a wee tumour ... a melanoma', they took it out, they said it was malignant, but ...'

'Jesus!' Brian interrupted. 'Are you all right?'

'I had chemo, ye know chemotherapy.'

'God, I thought I had problems, did you get the all clear?'

'Yeah I'm fine, I hope. Ye know, but I lost my own hair.'

'You sure?' he asked.

'The green light.'

'Jesus, I'm sorry, I didn't mean to offend you.'

'Well, I'm over it, I fought it, ye know, I have to get tests every once in a while, I'm clear I hope, for the moment, it's no big deal, it shouldn't come back.'

She touched her hair and looked into the drizzle outside the glass, falling on the heads of the shoppers. She sipped some coffee.

'I'm Jenny,' she said, turning to him.

He introduced himself.

'Well, is this what ye do? Sell cakes on Henry Street?' she asked pointing at the window.

'Yeah that's part of it, I've a bakery, it's a partnership, we found things tough for a while, we were in a bad way, we went out on the street to get cash, it's ...'

She leaned towards him.

'Yer good at it. Not bad at all actually, ye know, the sellin'.'

He looked at her and thought about something his grandmother had said about never letting a snake into your nest.

He was a little embarrassed.

'Well, I try, it's not easy, it's a living, some days are good, but ...'

He paused and smiled.

'Oh I saw ye a couple of weeks back standin' on yer trolley. Yer good at it'. She asked, 'do ye come out during the week?'

'No, Saturday afternoons. What do you do?'

'I'm in Trinity studyin' languages, French and Spanish, ye know.'

'You're from the North...your accent?'

She didn't react.

She stirred her coffee and asked him, 'Are ye married?'

He frowned.

'Yes.'

'Was that yer wife at the ball?

'That's where I saw you.' He leaned back recalling her in her white dress.

'Happy?' she asked, running her hand through her hair, staring into him.

'Yes, I've two children, yeah, I'm happy. Lucky, I suppose that she loves me at all ... we never seem to see each other.'

She lit a cigarette.

'You're very inquisitive,' he said.

'Yeah well.' she looked at the cigarette. 'I like to know, ye know, that's all.'

She smiled.

He stood up eyeing the door.

'Ah here's Frank. Frank!' he shouted.

His partner came over. Brian turned to the girl.

'Sorry.' he said trying to recall, 'I forgot your name ... I'm lousy on names.'

'Jenny ... I'm Jenny.'

'This is Frank, my partner.'

'How ye doin'?' she asked.

Frank nodded at her dismissively and turned to him.

'What's happened?'

'I lost it, around a corner, the whole lot, on the ground.'

'Did they get you?'

'No they left it, but I've had it for today, it's too wet, Frank you're soaked.'

'Yeah, yeah, are you okay?'

'Fine, I've had enough.'

'I'm going to clear them.' Frank said.

He stared at the girl.

'Don't get caught.' Brian said.

'Thanks.' He walked out but looked back at Brian and mouthed 'Don't you get caught.'

'He's nice.' she said.

'He likes coffee, you'll like him.'

'He seems, well, sincere.'

'Sincere, yeah I suppose so, I'll tell him you said that. That should surprise him.' He chuckled.

'Exactly' she said.

He watched her, her nails, her perfect turned-up nose, small lips, wild eyes and the gap between her two front teeth. He asked her if she was thirsty. She nodded. He thought about killing the snake, walking away from her eyes.

They drove to a pub nearby and drank Guinness. She told him about her father dying alone and her Protestant upbringing. They had about four pints and cut their histories. He told her he'd better get the crates back to the bakery and she asked if she could join him and as loose as hell in his mind, he told her he'd enjoy the company but as he drove he said, 'I'd better drop you off.'

Disappointed, she said 'Okay, yes, I understand, ye know,

that's okay ... exactly.'

He left her outside her flat on Lower Camden Street ... outside him.

She walked into her building and he stared at the driving wheel, rubbing it with his thumb. The rain stopped and the snake slithered across the water away from him. He thought he'd read somewhere about people who ate the snake's heart and drank its blood.

* * *

Brian and Frank were in the Cash and Carry. It had steel shelves packed with goods stacked to the ceiling.

Frank wheeled the trolley, steering it around the aisles. Brian walked beside him.

'Where's the fuckin' sugar? I want the 50-kilogram bags of castor, where the hell are they? They used to be here.' He turned to Brian.

'Look it's like this, if you let a woman sink her hook into you, you're fucked, you're better off pulling it out, losing a little flesh, and getting rid of her.'

His head moved around, examining the shelves.

'Where are those fuckin' bags kept anyway?' he shouted.

'Look', he continued, 'never let a woman get to you, they're like vampires, yeah, they come at you. Are you listening? They come at you, looking for your weak spot, if your dick is your weak spot, they know your dick is your weak spot, they know it, so they control it, then they control you. You've got to wear a parachute in a relationship.'

'Hold on Frank, listen, I've heard enough of this, you know it struck me today the way you go on, that basically you don't like women. That behind it all you are a misogynist.'

Frank wasn't listening.

'You need to know that you can jump out of that plane when you want to, you know when it's over, that's it, straight out that door. I always say, baby, this isn't the movies, this is real life. The next time it's goodbyeeeee! Otherwise they'll shoot you down in flames, you mark my words!'

Frank made an imitation dive and whistled. They reached the sugar.

'How many bags?'

'Three, hold on.'

Frank put his hand into his pocket and pulled out a bundle of cash.

'No, make it four.'

They started throwing large brown sacks of sugar onto the trolley. Frank continued acting it out, 'Frank you never write to me, you never send me notes, you know Frank, Xmas cards, little love notes, a birthday card would be nice.'

He stopped.

'You see Brian there's the hook all over again, the guilt number, I said to the last girl I was with, I said ...'

He tried to get serious, pointing his finger at a row of marmalade boxes.

'I said, "Baby, you come out with that shit once more and I'm going to leave, and I mean, leave, the parachute", 'I told her straight out.'

Brian walked around the corner with bags of raisins and placed them on the trolley.

'You're a ruthless cunt, Frank you know that?'

Frank moved close up to his face.

'Don't fool yourself, relationships are the same as a blind man thinking he's walking into a church, after a while he finds he's actually in a brothel, you never know what you're getting into, see what I mean, Brian, Brian where are you going?'

He'd headed off around the corner. Frank shouted after him, 'They're treacherous if you let them be. I'll give you an example of how to control them. I often say to a girl, look are you hungry? If she says "Yes" then I say, "I've just eaten".'

'You know something Frank, you don't need a partner, I've always said it about you, you need a fucking audience.'

Frank looked at him.

'Flour, how much do we need?'

'Ten bags soft, six wholemeal, no seven, we'll need another trolley, hold on I'll get it.'

At the flour rack Brian turned to him, the two of them standing there with fully-laden trolleys.

'Do you really like women?' he asked.

'I fucking love women.'

'You mean you love fucking women!'

'Yeah, well, it's all the same.'

Brian heaved bags of flour onto the second trolley.

'You're the type of guy that wrecks it for the rest of us, you know that Frank ... you're arrogant.'

'You're wrong. You see Brian, I'm not the same as you. I don't let them get to me, I go in with my eyes open and I can leave when I want to. That kind of logic comes with real intelligence.'

'Ha, intelligence, what has intelligence got to do with emotion?'

They came close to the till.

'Brian, emotion is intelligence, intelligence is logic. That's why racing stallions are so frisky. Real winners are highly sensitive, that's the way it is ... intelligence Brian ... Emotion Brian ... Logic ... Brian.'

'You know it all, don't you? Listen Frank, this may come as a surprise, but you're no Einstein.'

After they had loaded the van, Brian turned to him.

'Anyway, how many relationships have you had?'

Frank finished sorting out the bags and looked up.

'About thirty, yeah about thirty.'

Brian smiled as he sat into the van:

'Jesus, Frank you better make sure that parachute opens.'

* * *

June, late afternoon. The partners in the bakery drank pints of the black in the Galloping Green, a pub on the Stillorgan

Kissing the Orange

dual carriageway which brings Dublin's city traffic out to the South, Dun Laoghaire, Bray and on to Wicklow and the South East. In the corner of the pub, a TV showed the first week of Wimbledon.

As they drank, their imaginations fired up new proposals and as the alcohol coursed through, they became increasingly optimistic. Brian proposed visiting other banks. Frank resolved to return to the bakery that weekend and rehaul the oven and finally they both committed to lease new machinery, reliable machinery to increase their production.

Frank made a phone call and Brian left the pub high on hope and alcohol. The van was parked on the far side of the road and he crossed over the dual carriageway. He was in the centre aisle standing on the grass when the 84 bus slowed down and pulled up in front of him.

There was a girl in the back of the bus. Her hair stroked around her face, cut so that the ends of it licked her chin. She must have seen him because she had a startled look on her face. It was her, for sure. It was the girl. Jenny. The same smile he'd seen weeks back that had carried him to the edges of temptation.

The bus began to move away, impulsively he dashed across the road. The pitch diesel-smoke engulfed him as the bus accelerated. He sprinted after it, his jacket flapping. She looked back at him through the window.

There was a set of traffic lights and a line of cars backed up waiting for the red to change, the bus stopped. He reached it and hammered the glass. The driver shook his head and muttered. The hiss started and the doors opened.

'Jaysus!' said the driver 'I thought youse was going to leg it the whole way to Donnybrook station.'

'Thanks bud.' Brian said 'Thanks a lot.'

He pulled out a pound coin and placed it on the tray.

'Where are you going?' the driver asked.

He looked up, sucking in deep for his breath.

'Don't know yet ...'

'Smart, eh, go on.'

Brian turned to the faces staring at him and there she was with a scarf wrapped around her neck, laughing her head off.

'How ye doin?' she asked when she finished.

He sat beside her, gasping for breath. She could smell the drink from him.

'I have the van back at the pub, do you want a lift?'

'C'mon,' she said and stood up.

They got out at the next stop and walked back to the van. On the way he said, 'I've been thinking about you, I was going to call to your place ... I dropped it'.

'Exactly,' she said.

He cracked up.

He took the van across the winding roads of the Dublin mountains. They parked at the back of the bakery and he pulled the steel door open. He mimicked the word 'Exactly' in different accents, repeating it until she began to laugh.

She helped him with the crates, still smiling at his acting. He took the flour bags in and stacked them on the ground. He went out to the van and carried in the 50kg bags of castor sugar and the boxes of raisins. He was inside leaning over a steel table with a piece of paper, going through the invoice, ticking everything off and she started to bend over, moving boxes of raisins, showing off her legs and her ass. He pretended not to notice. She went to the table near him. She stood beside him. She could feel something from him. One minute she was looking at his nose, his eyes, the next his lips were over her and she was wrapped inside his arms. Her own eyes shut to the world, she opened her mouth and let the feeling wave, lost in time, fantasy and sensation. She fell back on a bag of flour, bursting it open with her weight, pushing the white powder over the floor. He was on her, the flour enveloping them both. She wrestled with the buckle of his belt as she felt his hand up under her skirt peeling down her knickers. She wanted him, she felt him enter, yes, oh yes, inside her.

Kissing the Orange

The ecstasy as he went into her. Her legs, her hair, her shoulders and flour coating them and her floating away on a sea of white powder. She was silent with it. It had been so long since she had felt a man and she wanted it, even when she had it, more. She felt right about it. Her hips up and her nails in, clawing deep.

She wanted more and she wanted less and more and less and more and she didn't care and he was kissing her the whole time. She was sure he had never touched anyone with such a passion, no, not like this. She was sure this beat was for her, really for her, for the two of them and the fierce tension of his body made her happy, so very happy. She drifted away. Wrapped in sweat and lust they struggled for each other, the pleasure of conquest, submission and the fulfilment of instinct.

She said 'yes.'
She said 'yes.'
She said 'yes.'

* * *

The beat started that week through the crystals of rain in her, in him. Irresistible, unbounded, a pulse of emotion. The beat that you are never conscious of until you try to feel for it, touch it, feeding your imagination, slow simple bass without substance yet with all substance, total in its invisibility, empty, yet at the very same time, a chorus of sound growing and dying. The centre of it like the atrium of the heart, all encompassing, its walls, gentle yet powerful.

You never know when it is going to start. Who will give it to you? Where you will find it? The beat of Love, Danger, Sex, Attraction, Fate and Destiny.

She knew that it had started. Sometime later in bed, smoking one of her Silk-Cuts, encircled in the bubble of warmth they had created with their lovemaking, she turned and said, 'Ye know I saw ye at the Trinity Ball and I felt somethin'. I couldn't put my finger on it, ye know. But after I spoke to ye on Henry Street, that first time with yer hair all wet, I knew, I knew.'

He said,'My defences came down, you cut through walls. The last thing I needed was to see weakness, especially my own.'

She said 'When we make love, I forget myself. But it's more. It's as if I'm looking at myself through everythin' with ye, as if somethin' out there is puttin' us together, watchin'. It's eerie'.

'When you said 'exactly', Jesus, I laughed, but inside I was nervous, I haven't been that nervous since I met Ciara.'

Then she said it: 'Yer wife, she's really beautiful, ye know.' Her lack of jealousy surprised him, he couldn't believe that someone could let it go like that.

* * *

Valerie was born in Devon, moved with her parents from England to Belfast when she was seven and lived there ever since. She studied in Belfast and travelled to Dublin to see bands in the Baggot and spend time with Jenny.

Jenny, on many occasions, had to reason with Valerie's insistence. Often they had been in night-clubs, restaurants or even back in school when she found her friend staring at her in that way, making her uncomfortable, unsure.

When Jenny rejected her, Valerie tried to hurt her, taking a strange revenge but nonetheless she loved the girl because she'd been around during her bad time when she needed someone. After she underwent chemotherapy, Valerie had been utterly caring, sacrificing her own schedule to give Jenny support, coming to the Belfast City Hospital every day, laughing her into health when there had been no-one else. Always strong for her, holding her hand when her hand was cold, filling the vacuum when the emptiness was overpowering.

Valerie. A girl-friend who sat near her in school, someone who grew up with her, close, talked her through her first period and what it would be like when they both had babies. Valerie who'd joked with her in school about the really funny hairs that had started to grow and curl into circles and neither of them could understand it and when Jenny's breasts started and kept going and the laughter about all the truck drivers who would slow down. Valerie who'd helped her through her sickness with time and love.

She met Jenny's sister, Rachel, over by the Castlecourt Shopping Centre in the centre of Belfast. After some small talk Rachel cut to the quick.

'Someone said she's met a man.'
'And how do you know?'
'Ireland's small, ye know.'
'It's true, she really likes him.'
Rachel asked heavily accented.
'Have ye seen him yerself?'
'No, she seems happy. I spoke to her on the phone,' and continued 'Well, it's true, I know from her voice, the way she told me, it's the real thing this time, she seems so well, happy, but I'll be going to Dublin soon enough to sort it out.'

Rachel turned and walking away said: 'Ye'd better cos if he's a fuckin' Taig, there'll be trouble, ye tell her that.'

*

Valerie wears one of her amazing hats. A beret with badges pinned onto it.
'I don't know what I'm going to do with my life.'
'Yer a product of the system Val, ye got all yer school exams, ye went to college to study law, yer a clone of yer mother. Ye have her insecurities, and now ye tell me ye don't know what yer going to do. Cop onto yerself!'
'How can you say all that? How could I be your best

friend if I was that much of a clone? Anyway my mother can't stand you.'
'So what!'
'I'm only telling you.'
'Listen Val, I want to get on with my life, ye have to find something that ye believe in besides politics and yer Dad and Mum and all their wee baggage.'

*

'Jen, I can't make up my mind about anything.'
'There's only one thing ye need in life that matters.'
'What?'
'Courage, Val, courage.'
'You were always so strong. Behind the hats, I'm so inhibited.'
'Val, ye should come out and tell the world yer a lesbian, and the confidence will build from there.'
'In Belfast, are you crazy? It's not that simple.'
Valerie lights a cigarette.
'It wouldn't matter if you went back to Cornwall, ye'll only find happiness when ye come to terms with yer feelin's.'
'Don't mention England. I love Belfast . . . I love you'.
'Val, ye have me . . . ye have every part of me except my body and my body is only one wee part of me.'
'I know Jen but I really love you, I want to be near you.'
'Listen Val this isn't good, yer like a wee terrier my father used to have, ye don't know when to let go. Anyway it's a crush for ye, just a crush!'

*

'Anyway Jen, what's wrong with kissing a girl?'
'Nothing, I never said there was anythin' wrong. I

never said there was anythin' wrong, ye know, just leave me out of the picture.'
Valerie takes a sip of her Vodka and tonic.
'Jen, kissing a girl is a lot nicer than kissing a guy.'
'How would ye know?'
'I've kissed guys, they're all hairy, they leave rashes all over me.'
'Well that's the way I like it, I've told ye before, why don't ye hang out with a load of girls and keep me as a friend, anyway I don't want yer tongue or any other girl's down my throat.'

*

'Jen, Jen, I've met someone, someone really nice.'
'Thank God, who is she?'
'She's English, she's from Hounslow, it's on the Piccadilly line.'
'Is she nice?'
'Love at first sight, Jen, I'm so happy, she's really nice, really special.'
'I'm so happy for ye, I'm so happy Val, don't get yer heart broken, ye know.'
Jenny gives her a hug.
'Make sure ye keep in touch with me.' she says.
'I will, don't worry Jen, I love you Jen.'
'I love ye too Val.'

*

'I've fallen for someone.'
'I know you Jenny and I know he's married, am I right?'
There is a pause.
'Yes, yer right, ye always know.'
'If he makes you happy, I'm happy. You never wanted

a relationship, you always wanted affairs.'
'Yes, I know, I wonder why I can't meet someone my own age.'
'Me?'
'Don't start Val.'
'You want excitement, that's your thing, you're afraid of death.'
'Don't be ridiculous.'
'I'm not, you've always been the same, even at school you always did mad things to get the adrenalin going.'

*

'Val why am I so crazy?'
'You could have died if that cancer had spread, now you want to live.'
'Yes, maybe that's it.'
'It is Jen, with you it was always living on the edge, now you're worse.'
'Ye don't hold it against me, do ye?'
'I wouldn't be here, would I, if I did?'
'Ye know what I mean.'
'Don't be silly.'

*

She says to Valerie.
'At last it's true, I'm kissin' the man I want.'
'Do your family know?'
'I don't care, I don't care, ye know.'
'You better watch it, I won't tell them. You're my friend Jen, I'd never do that.'

*

Sometime later they go out and Valerie tells her that it's over with the English girl and the two girls embrace.
Locked in compassion, tears, retribution, understanding, love and hope against years of solitude.
A very close bond.

* * *

They met. Brian greeted her.
'Hi Kiddo.'
'How' ye doin?' she asked.
They opened the door to McDaids in Harry Street and the swirl of smoke sucked them in. They passed the regulars at the bar and sat in one of the wooden cubicles, beside them, nicotine-stained walls, creamy and brown as a sour pint.

She took his tie and put it around her own neck, it dangled in a triangle. She told him the story of Mr Jackson. The school teacher from Derry who used to come into the classroom and all the girls who flirted with him, trying to make him embarrassed.

She was the worst. Oh yes she had played his eyes. She'd fancied him right enough. At the debs he came to her table and bent towards her and she could see the thinning hair and in front of all the others he asked her to dance. She was thrilled. Nobody would see any space between them. She didn't give a damn. The house captain, who'd fancied him from the start, who'd even written love letters to him, wet her knickers when Jenny took Mr Jackson's hand and the poor girl in her dress ready for him and Jenny and him waltzing through eyes of envy.

Brian laughed at the story, laughed so much that she knew at that moment that she could live with him. The same as her, yes she could live and laugh with him through and through.

Then she told him that as soon as she touched the teacher the fantasy blew away, like a death it never returned, just haunted her.

'Let's get pissed.' she said.

Later when they were drunk in Grafton Street, she leaned up to his ear and kissed him and he smiled, loving it, yeah, really loving it and she said, 'Ye always get what ye want, yer like a little boy, yer a wee baby!'

And later 'Yer always early'.

'Yeah, I know I suppose being in business teaches you all that, people learn to trust your time, it's a sort of progression.'

'It sounds so practical comin' from yeu, I think yer a good timekeeper, it's inherited, probably from yer father's side.'

She smiled at him.

'Yeah, I got it from the same place you got your accent,' he said.

'Do I ask too many questions?'

He shrugged.

'Ye never talk about yer wife.' she said.

'I don't want to, it's . . . I don't want to.'

'That's okay, I understand.'

'You're unbelievable, you don't have jealousy in you, do you?' he said.

She looked out of the car window and the thought crossed her mind that a man should have as many lovers as he wants and that her own father was a victim of order and the rule-book and that she would have liked him to have had someone, anyone to stop his loneliness turning into alcoholism.

* * *

The bay windows of her flat overlooked Lower Camden Street. Sometimes when she opened them it was as though she was letting in the street traders from below. There was a bakery next door and in the mornings she could smell the bread being cooked, the aroma wafting around her room. At times she felt she was in a Parisian side street and all she needed was the wheeze of an accordion and good coffee, ground out, thick and aromatic.

Sometimes she used to take it easy, going to the library, instilling the memory of the aroma and the pictures in her mind. If she was there in the afternoons and the wind blew in the right direction she could hear the traders outside selling off their produce. Some days there were apples all over the flat, apples in the bath, between the taps, on the bathroom sink, the mantelpiece. Apples everywhere. Other days it was cabbages. Beetroot, Bananas, Peaches, she didn't care. She bought on impulse, she lived on impulse. Her life was impulse.

Sometimes in the morning she tripped off downstairs and talked to the traders as they stacked up their stalls.

Mrs Walsh, Marie Healy, the O'Donovan sisters. She'd talk to them as if she'd known them her whole life.

Some days after the rain when she saw they were a bit down, overladen with stock, she'd put on one of her wigs and give them a little show. They all knew her, they all knew her tricks, her temper and her fierce capacity for affection.

The walls of her flat were covered with the posters of animals and rock stars. On the mantelpiece there was a framed photograph of her father, a stern but honest face with a gentleness about the eyes. In front of the window all her wigs balanced on small wooden poles. A blonde piece with the hair trickling to the floor, another auburn and then a short black wig cut so that the ends curled up to where her nose would be, on the window sill a huge brown wig with curls, bushy and wild and beside it a bleached wig, short and neat.

* * *

He was in a chair sipping coffee looking at the curl of Jim Morrisson's smile. She put on the music, picked up an apple and began to bite into it. She chewed each piece of it slowly and watched him. She finished the fruit and placed the core on a table and started to try on the wigs. After each one she went to the bathroom, checked herself, came out and gave him a little twirl. He laughed and clapped and asked for more. She came out with her auburn wig and it falling like a mane about her back. One by one she put them all on.

Finally, she came out of the bathroom with a blue wig and dressed top to toe in blue, with the shined blue shoes and blue gloves up to her elbow.

'Jesus!' he said 'you look amazing.'

'Ye see Brian, ye think ye know me, but I can change my colours the same as a wee chameleon.'

She threw an apple to him. 'Some night I'll put on my orange gear for ye.'

'Thank you,' he said catching it.

'Don't thank me,' she giggled. 'Thank God, ye met me.'

That was the first time she said that and he thought how different she was from all the other women in Dublin and he hoped she'd never change.

* * *

The twelfth of July, about one o'clock in the morning. The night air ran bitter. Brian had finished in the bakery. He drove hard to meet her, he moved quick through time.

Nothing mattered but the girl. She had become him. She was his life. He was her. In his eyes there was madness, his madness, her madness, their madness, their beat.

He wiped his forehead with his knuckles and cleaned the sweat across the leg of his jeans. He charged through the gears, making a left into Clanbrassil Street and stopped at a traffic light. He rolled down the window. Cool air rushed through. He put on the radio. A reporter talked about the North. The Orange marches that had started, the Lower Ormeau Road, the playing of 'The Sash', the Lambeg Drums, the accordion bands, the bonfires, the R.U.C. riot squads, the District Masters, the Loyalists, Unionists, Ian Paisley, the Orange Lodge. He switched it off.

He made a turn by Christ Church Cathedral, past the queue outside Leo Burdock's, the chipper, and cut through South Great George's Street. A girl ran across him fleeing from her own insanity and cut across in front of the car. Her eyes flashed fear. He hit the brakes hard narrowly missing her.

'Jesus!'

He pulled the car over and opened the door and gulped in breaths of air, knowing that he had been driving too fast. An empty milk carton tumbled past him. He breathed evenly, smelling the hops from Thomas Street. He restarted the engine and slammed it into gear and drove through the intersection with Kevin Street and on into Lower Camden Street.

Was she there? He looked towards the window of her flat. The light was on. He found a tight space, reversed into it and got out. He ran to the front door of the building and put the key into the brass Yale. The lock clicked open. He climbed up the concrete stairs and inserted a key into a second lock.

A big light.

He looked into the living room and Jenny stood in front of a turf fire, a blanket wrapped around her shoulders and she let it fall from her and crossed her arm over her breasts, her pubic hairs sequinned against the white of her thighs.

She smiled at him. The biggest smile for him. The biggest smile of all.

He looked unsure. She dropped her hand, motioning for him to come for her.

'I saw ye parkin', I've missed yeu,' she said.

He switched off the light. He moved towards her without words. He grasped her breasts and put his mouth over her lips.

The fire flickered light across the room, around them and over her skin giving it the look of peach and warmth and love and surrender.

She stroked his hair, ran her fingers through the buttons of his shirt and in a time when the expectation became unbearable for her she unbuckled his belt. He pulled her down onto the rug in front of the fire. She gripped him and guided him into her wetness. He penetrated deep inside her, her legs rose high and her fingers dug into his back almost cutting the skin. He rode her filling all her impatient longings. Her eyes closed. For a moment they stopped kissing while he rose away from her, her hips rose with him. Then he emptied himself into her and she whispered into his ear, 'I hate yer guts, I hate yer guts, I hate yer guts!'

This was the place. The place of love. The fuck. Everything. As they fell into the abyss of satisfaction she held him tight, put her lips to his ear and whispered,

'And I love ye, love ye, love ye.'

The beat.

* * *

'Brian, I weighed myself today, I'm over nine stone. Are you listenin'.
He looks at her.
'Well, big deal.'
'Well!' she says pinching his nose and sitting on his lap 'What's it like goin' out with a wee fat pig?'

*

They're in her flat.
He goes over to the fridge, pulls out a beer and clips open the can.
'Here Kiddo!' he says, putting the can down hard on the table in front of her.
She folds her arms and says, 'Sometimes ye can be so rude.'
'I'm only giving you a beer, so?'
'Well, I'd never turn around to ye and say, "Ay shithead, yer wee coffee's made".'
'I didn't say that.'

'Well that's what it sounded like.'

*

She is smoking and makes one of her salads, throwing in slices of garlic and onions.
'Sometimes ye don't know how lonely it feels.'
'I do.'
'Ye don't, ye know.'
'Listen I'm living this as much as you.'
She comes over to him and blows smoke into his face, the way she always does when she has something hard to deliver.
'Well, let's look at it this way, is yer bed warm when ye get home?'

*

Looking into the mirror, she says. 'I have angel's lips and the devil's ass.'
'Who says?' *Brian asks.*
'An old boyfriend.'
'You just need reassurance.'
'Re-assurance, I know I'm good lookin'.'
'You're cocky, I'll give you that.'
'I can get any man I want, ye know'.
She turns to him and wriggles her bum at the same time and it seems to him sure enough, the devil's ass.

*

'Was I crazy to let ye know I love ye?'
'No.' *he said.*
'Well, why are ye treatin' me so bad?'
'Look. Here's the money, grab a taxi.' *he barks.*
'I don't want yer money.'

'Look I have a lot on my mind I don't need this.' he says.
'Don't ye dare talk to me like that.'
She hits him hard on the cheek with her fist.
He starts to laugh.
She flails at him hitting him with both fists. 'Go on Jenny, beat it, I'll talk to you tomorrow, and by the way,' he smiles, 'I hate your guts.'
He's still laughing.
She clenches her teeth and turns around.
He slaps her bottom.
'Bastard!' she says.
'Oh, touchy.'
He smiles into her.

*

'Yer crazy Brian, yer as crazy as me, I need ye. I need ye crazy.'
He runs his fingers through her hair.
'What is it Brian? I can't understand it.'
'I don't know Jen, I'm basically a creep, and a two-timing good for nothing.'
But she covers his mouth and bends over to whisper in his ear, 'Yes, but yer mine, all mine'.

*

He says, 'You know a man with a little discipline, a little courage, and a little pride can easy make his mark.'
'God forgive me Brian, but yer too fond of the women.'

*

She puts on a sash bringing it across her shoulders and over her blouse.
'My uncle died and my mother gave it to me — do you like it!'
'Jesus, Jenny, put it away will you.'
'Well, I like it, I'm really proud of it .... I don't care what you think.'

*

It's raining.
He lights one of his huge fires, the entire room reflects speckled light.
The perfume of turf-smoke filling their nostrils.
They've finished making love.
Opposite each other in front of the fire.
He looks at the light coming off her face.
Now it is a time of closeness.
He leans back and watches her smoking a cigarette.
'Why don't you stop?' he says.
'I'll stop when ye give me an orgasm.' she replies.
'Do you want it wrapped?'
'Maybe.'
She points between her legs 'Ye better get to work on that.'
'Maybe you should start riding a bike or a horse or something.' he jokes.
'Funny.' she says 'I was thinkin' about that the other day.'
'Do you ever stop thinking about that?'
'I have a healthy appetite, ye know. I can't help it, I suppose I'm just horny.'
'Yeah, for cigarettes and pints.' he laughs.
'Ye never want to admit defeat, ye always have to have the last word, don't ye?'
But she's putting her fingers to her crotch opening

her pinkness up to him.
He moves into her with his tongue.
'Come on, lick me Brian, lick me to death.'
She lies back groaning.

*

'Do ye believe in the Devil?' she asks.
'You mean the tail and all that shit.'
'I think if yer bad, ye know, evil, that...'
'That what?'
'That ye'll go to hell.'
'And then what?' he's laughing.
She lights two matches together.
'Burn baby, burn.' she's serious.

*

'I was going to ring you.' he says.
'Yeah sure, well ye know I can't ring yeu, so I wait, all the time like an actress cooped up in a cheap Hollywood flat waitin' for the phone to ring.'
'I never said it was going to be a telephone relationship.'
'Ye didn't ring ... ye know ... I waited in last night.' she says.
'The whole world doesn't revolve around you.'
'How could it when yer my world? And when yer gone I'm so alone, if ye want a mistress, ye have to treat me the same way ye would treat a real person.'
She blows rings of smoke into his face.
'Oh a real person is it, did I say you were a robot? Sometimes I can't ring and that's it, I just can't.'
'Keep in contact with me, ye know, that's all.' she says.

'Oh, oh here we go.'
'Fuck you!' she says and leaves.

* * *

He called. They went to O'Donoghues in Merrion Row and sat in a snug. The barman in a white apron set up the pints. Jenny was ravenous and munched crisps.

'Get me another packet, will ye?'

'You love your food.'

'Well it's cold, I can't stop eatin', it's so cold. It must be the worst summer ever, this rain, ye know, it's gettin' to me.'

Brian went over to the bar and came back with her crisps, she saw a woman sitting at the bar and it reminded her of something, the way she sat there.

'My mother had a mastectomy last year.'

'That's breasts isn't it?' he asked.

'Yes, only one, but ye know she blamed it on Dad, on the pressure of the divorce, she blamed everythin' on him.'

'What do you mean?' he asked.

She took some Guinness and stared into his face.

'He was a lot older than her ... my dad, he was ... ah, anyway age doesn't matter .'

'Who are you telling?'

'Well yer only thirty-four, there was twenty five years between them.'

'Age' he muttered.

'She never really talks much about it, about them', she interrupted. 'Dad told me that she was very rebellious, that was it, he didn't want to say a bad word about her, he never did, he used to say that when people shook his hand they knew where they stood, that's the way he was.'

Jenny drifted away. Her eyes wet with the memory. He put his arm around her. She looked into him and felt something.

'Ye know?' she said 'He never really had it in him to talk badly about anyone, he used to say if ye don't have somethin' good to say about someone ... don't say it.'

'What did he do?'

'He was a vet in Kilrea, in the beginning she used to work there in the surgery then she lost interest. Then he started drinkin' to kill the boredom. Kilrea is a small town.'

'Where is it?' he asked.

'It's a tiny place on the River Bann, the customers came from all over, he was a good vet. I sometimes wonder, if he hadn't drank so much ... '

Her voice trailed off.

'There's no harm in a few pints Jenny.' Brian said.

'I'd really hate ye to take that road, it's too dark, too destructive, too addictive.'

'Look who's talking.'

But he seemed surprised by her care.

'You never talk about your mother.' he said to her.

'Oh, I...' she trailed off.

'Your mother?' he pushed.

'Well, she and I don't get on, ye know ... the only thing we have in common is our religion.'

She went silent, after some time she continued.

'Actually, I really hate her, she's vicious, sometimes she hits me, can ye imagine, once I went with a lad from Ballymena, he was really nice...'

'What happened?'

'He was married.'

'Oh, another one!'

'It's not what ye think, I knew him before ... he was only twenty-two, but she, well she went mad when she found out ... and he wasn't even Catholic.'

'How mad?'

'She really killed me, ripped out my hair, ye know when I had hair, kicked me, Wallace helped her.'

'Wallace!'

'That's her man, Wallace, he's a bastard, he helped her, he's a real bastard.'

Kissing the Orange

She looked into him, the pint glass tight in her fist, she knew what she had said was vital. Later as he drove her home, she said:

'He's dangerous, Brian.'

'He's a hard man then?'

'He's dangerous, he doesn't have to be hard, he's, well ...'

'Go on.'

'He doesn't drink, smoke, he's into discipline, a real control freak, a real hard bastard. Bikes, football tattoos, that shit...he lives on fear.'

'What is he? Tell me, what are we talking about here? Has he done time?'

She stared straight through him.

'Yeah.'

'Well?'

'The Maze.'

He drove a while and opened the window, breathing in air.

'Jesus!'

'I told ye, ye don't know him.'

'I know that when someone's been inside they don't want to go back.'

'Ye don't know him Brian, ye don't know him. Our house in Dundonald has bullet proof windows ... ye understand?'

Brian turned silent. She talked in a soft, pained voice.

'They gave me a lot of hassle before I came here, wouldn't let me come down, it was terrible, before he died my father had wanted me to go to Trinity, she wanted me in Queen's. It was bad, He got involved, she used bring him into our place, when Dad and myself stayed together and he'd sit and stare at me, my Dad was really gentle. He used to intimidate him, if ye only knew what that man has done!'

'How high is he in the organisation?'

'I shouldn't have got involved with ye.'

He looked into her.

'Listen, Jenny ...' he trailed off.

'Let's leave it. I don't want to talk about it, anyway I love ye ... That's what matters ... nothin' else matters.'

Later that evening.

'Listen', he said, 'I want to tell you out straight, I love my wife.'

'I'll never ask ye to leave her.'

'I needed you to know. I don't want you getting any illusions.'

'Don't worry, I know anyway, I don't mind sharin' ye, jus' be straight with me.'

'I'll always be straight, always.'

'I know,' she said 'That's why I'm here.'

That night when she went to bed she wondered whether she should have told Brian all those things. She stared at her posters of Curt Cobain and felt the honest wildness coming back at her. She watched flies circling the light which hung from the ceiling. She watched a spider crawl into a corner and spin its web. She imagined Brian and herself trapped in the threads waiting for Wallace to eat them.

She needed sleep and she couldn't find that place. She smoked through the dark, trying to keep away the smell of fear that their conversation had evoked.

In the small hours as she listened to the cars outside, she felt as though her father's eyes were on her, as though he was trying to tell her she was repeating the same mistakes that he himself had made, as though he was trying to warn her to be careful.

That night for the first time her conscience drowned her in a sea of questions. But she knew if she kept it going from there on in that it was going to last. She would make sure. She was not going to lose him, the same way she'd lost everyone and everything else.

* * *

Two nights later.

'You're snoring.'

She didn't wake.

'You're snoring.'

He nudged her.

'Huh.'

She started to wipe her eyes.

'You're snoring, I said.'

'Sorry.'

'You're snoring,' he repeated.

She began to move, her head emerged out from under the blankets.

'Brian, what are ye doin' ?'

He was out of the bed fiddling about the floor looking for something.

'Where's my watch? Where are my clothes? Jesus what's the time? where am I?'

'What do ye mean? Yer here with me, what do ye mean where are ye?'

'What time is it? God, my head!'

He searched for his watch.

'God, I'm wrecked, where's the light switch? Jesus ... I'm thirsty'. He reached over to a small glass of water and drank the contents.

'Was there something in there?' he asked.

'Where?'

'In the glass.'

'Did yeu drink from that glass ... my lenses ... my contact lenses ... Jesus ... ye drank my lenses.' She charged out of the bed.

'I never knew you wore lenses ... I didn't know ... I thought I felt something.'

'My lenses, my lenses ... you drank my lenses', she began to beat him.

'Hey easy' he said, 'I didn't know.'

She stormed out of bed, lifted the glass up and shouted, 'I

don't believe it'. She marched to the bathroom and screamed in rage behind the door.

He put on the light and found the timepiece, turned it upside down and stared at it.

'Jesus, it's not eleven?'

He turned the watch the right way around.

'It's five, fuckin' hell, I'm gone,' he shouted.

Jenny came back in and began looking for cigarettes.

'Time, Time, Time!' she cried.

'It's always the fuckin' same with ye, always time, ye can't spend one night with me without lookin' at that watch, it's like a ... like a child screamin' at ye for a bottle!'

'I'm sorry Jenny ... how was I to know?' he said, leaning over to the bedside table.

She sat down and began to smoke. When she'd cooled down she said, 'Why don't ye leave and let me finish my fuckin' cigarettes.'

He tied his laces, laughing to himself about it all. The wigs, the lenses, he wondered whether she was real at all and then he realised that in a strange way he was attracted to her vulnerability.

He looked at her and said, 'Those fags are making you snore.'

He stood up, took his jacket from a chair. She screamed after him:

'Leave me alone!'

She picked up a mug beside the bed and threw it at him. It hit the wall and smashed into pieces. He turned around.

'Jenny, you'll have to do something about your aim.'

'Go to yer fuckin' wife!' she screamed at him, 'and you better buy me glasses.'

* * *

It was early evening. They drove to Dun Laoghaire and walked along the west pier. The *Granuaile* was moored. People strolled the pier, there were dogs, children, joggers, couples and the old with walking sticks. They listened to the 'clink', 'clink' of the taut ropes against the yachts' masts. They walked to the sun-dial. She glanced at him and took his hand.

'I'm sorry for behavin' like a, like an idiot, I...'

He cut her short.

'Yeah, it's okay ... It was my fault ... I'll have to buy you some glasses.'

'I'm sorry.'

'Stop saying sorry, you lost the head, that's all, it's good, it means you care enough to lose it.'

'I don't know what's up with me.'

'Jesus, Jenny, stop apologising, it's okay, I've forgotten about it.'

They looked at each other and laughed.

They reached the sun-dial and walked around it, examining the brass engravings inlaid into the ceramic squares. They left it and walked the pier towards the Lighthouse. They passed a memorial, she touched the inscription, running her fingers over the smooth granite. She had a feeling that it would all end suddenly, she sensed the brutality of an unexpected death. She smelt the sea, he turned to her.

'I don't know what you see in me.'

'Plenty ... Brian.'

'You're nuts to want a married man.'

'I don't see it that way, ye know.'

They walked for a while.

'How long do you think we've got?'

'Forever.' she said.

'Don't be ridiculous Jenny. Be realistic, events overtake.'

She paused, looked out to the water covering the rocks and thought he was reading her mind.

'I'll make it last, ye know ... I'll make it last.'

They strolled back and as they neared the life-boat house, she said to him, 'Brian I mean it, I'll make it last.'

When they reached the boathouse, she pulled his head

down with her hand behind his neck and touched his lips with her fingers, running them across his grin, around his nose, over his eyes until she had engrained all his features into her mind.

'Give us a kiss. A wee Irish kiss.'

'I'll give you two kisses.' he said 'And I'll kiss the Orange in you.'

He leaned down. He covered her lips until she felt that she existed only for that moment on the pier, that that moment would forever be with her, by her and in her, she felt droplets of rain on the skin of her forehead and she felt so happy.

* * *

She's vegetarian.
She loves animals.
She tells him that she loves horses, dogs, fish, insects, everything that lives, that her dad taught her to work with them, to know them, respect nature's way.
When he asks her in some restaurant, would she like some steak or a little fish, she gets really angry, 'I never eat my friends, never, never, never.'

*

One afternoon they're in Bewley's sitting opposite each other.
A man in a suit is beside them, reading his paper and eating a cake.
A wasp comes in, hovers around them and lands on a sugared bun.
The man rolls up his paper and in one swipe brings it down on the insect killing it.
Jenny horrified, grabs the newspaper out of the man's hand and starts hitting him around the head,

shouting, 'Don't ye kill my friends, don't ye kill my friends, ye big bully'.

*

They're in St. Stephen's Green and she sees a duck hobbling along on one leg beside the pond.
She gets really upset.
He frowns bemused.

*

'Ye know when I die, I'm goin' to come back as a goldfish, I know it. Ye know, ye should never hurt yer friends, and especially ye should never eat yer friends.' she says.
He says 'You're wearing leather shoes, where do you think they came from?'
'Fuck ye, Brian O'Neill, ye know exactly what I mean.'
'Oh all right.'

* * *

Jenny cooked pasta. She had finished on the phone with her mother. She was full of tension and hormones and a fight. He sat at the table looking at the posters, then he looked up at the window at the rain against the glass.

'When's your birthday?'

'The twenty-second of May, why do ye ask?' she replied without turning around

He opened a page of the paper.

'You're a Gemini, doesn't that mean you've a dual personality?'

'That's the devil's talk, I don't believe in horoscopes.'

'I suppose your mother says that.'

'What?'

'That ... the devil's talk, you're always saying it, it's so, I don't know, anti pagan or something as though you think everyone else is nuts.'

'Well, ye are.'

'And where do you fit in?' he asked, 'You're twice as bad.'

'Listen, Brian I'm not goin' to have a row with ye, I'm not in the mood. Shut up and smoke yer cigar.'

'You Anglo-saxons are all the same, repressed emotion, you're a typical Prod, it's all locked in, all Orange, you should have listened to yourself talking to your mother on the phone, it's pathetic. All control and perverted logic. Jesus, you'll start beating the Lambeg Drum next.'

'Who do ye think yer talkin' to, generalisin' that way. I'm proud of my heritage. It's my past, my life yer talkin' about.'

'It's true and I notice the way you don't want to pay for anything, I'll bet your mother taught you that.'

'I pay my way, how dare you.'

'You never pay for anything when you're with me.'

'How dare ye, how dare ye. I'm broke, ye know, I'm on a wee allowance, ye know that, ye bastard!'

She took a bundle of saucers and threw them at him.

'Fuck ye!' she screamed.

One of the plates hit him on the forehead above his right eye, hurting him. He stood up.

' ... totally dependent, you don't even realise it, dependent on your mother for your flat, on me for your drinks.'

'And where do ye get yer sex from? Ye bastard.'

'I can get that at home.'

'Fuck ye, the truth comes out now.'

'Well you knew that from the start, you knew what the terms were, no strings.'

She picked up a plate and hurled it, then a second and a third. He ducked and side-stepped as they crashed about him.

'Do ye think I'm going to be yer mistress forever, ye little creep,' she bawled at him.

Kissing the Orange

He touched his forehead with his shirt and said:

'You mark my words, you'll end up marrying a Prod, a true Orange Prod, your own kind, he'll probably be a 'Billy' an' all straight from plantation stock, you should hear yourself on the phone.'

'What are ye sayin'? I'll tell ye one thing, it's goin' to be a lot better than marryin' a two-timin' Catholic like yeu with no morals and a wee fuckin' hypocrite and ye think ye can go to confession and bow and scrape to the Pope and everythin's all right again, ye little weak Fenian fuck'.

She picked up a large dinner plate and threw it. It hit the wall and smashed into tiny pieces.

'You know something, sometimes I think you reckon you're one notch above the rest of us,' he said.

'Ye bastard, look at ye. How dare ye!'

She hurled a mug and a saucepan at him.

'Ye little fucker, ye can't commit to anything, ye piss me off, yer not straight to me or yer wife, yer full of lies, it's no wonder yer life's a mess, and ye think I'm better than ye, I am, ye miserable cheap lyin' bastard.'

She bent down to where the empty wine bottles were stacked, pulled one out and threw it across the room. It hit the door, bounced back and rolled over the floor.

'Jesus, Jenny take it easy, take it easy, calm down, you'll have nothing left in the place.'

'Dependent on ye, dependent on ye.' she screamed 'Get out of my flat, get out of here ... stay out of my life. I've got pride ... ye bastard ... pride!'

She picked up some more empty wine bottles and tossed them. They sailed across the room and splintered into pieces of glass. She picked up anything she could lay her hands on. The floor was littered with glass, broken delph, cutlery and pots and her fierce temper. He reached the door and turned around, touching his wound.

'I can see this is not one of your better days.'

She screamed, 'Fuuuck off!'

Another bottle flew past his shoulder, down the staircase and hit the stone floor breaking into fragments. He reached the street but as he was about to cross the road, a head of cabbage sailed past him and she screamed 'Bastard!' from the window.

He turned and shouted out, 'See you tomorrow!'

'Bastard ... I fuckin' hate ye.'

One of the traders went over to him.

'You leave our Jen alone!'

He laughed.

'She's great, isn't she? You wouldn't think she had a temper, would you?'

'Leave her alone! She's in the horrors, leave her be.'

* * *

Ciara prepared dinner. She took a saucepan from the cooker and spooned the contents out onto a large serving plate and carried them over to the table. He sat down. On his left-hand side Michael banged a spoon on the table, on his right Eileen read a holiday brochure that her mother had picked up. Michael looked up.

'Daddy, will God make it a nice day tomorrow, like will he stop all the rain?'

'He will, darling, he will.' Brian replied.

He laughed. Ciara suggested that they go to dancing lessons.

'C'mon Ciara, I can'y dance mon,' in a mock Scottish accent.

'You were pretty good in my day.' she said.

'But that was different, that was disco, strutting my stuff, yo.'

He stood up and did a turn. She went over to him and put an olive between his teeth.

'You can do it. Remember the Trinity Ball!' she insisted.

'Anyway it would be good for us, all you do when you

come home is watch TV.'

'What nights are we talking about.'

'Mondays, maybe Thursday's, if you're good enough.'

She winked at Eileen, took a salad bowl from the side dresser and filled it with iceberg lettuce from the sink. She turned to him.

'You know, it would be good for us, that's all I'm saying'.

She noticed him frowning.

'Brian, please, I've always wanted to, I've never had a partner.'

'You mean Glenn Miller and all that stuff at the Trinity Ball don't you?' he asked.

She started to spoon out the food onto the children's plates.

After he'd helped himself, he said:

'I love the way you feed us.'

'What do you mean?' she asked.

'Your cooking is good, you never burn a thing and it always tastes great, the bread, sauces, pastas, you know what... you cook with love, that's it, that's why it tastes good, you cook with love.'

'Thanks Brian, that's really kind, now stop trying to get off the subject, how about the dancing. Will you do it?'

He took a mouthful of lettuce so that it was all over his face. His daughter Eileen laughed. He put it in, crunched for a moment and said:

'Mondays and Thursdays, yeah okay.'

Ciara came over to him and kissed him.

'What's that for?'

'I don't know, I suppose I felt like it.'

'You see kids, all you have to do is say yes.'

He opened his arms to his wife.

'So when do you want to start?'

'Well, the first lesson is next week.'

'Okay, in at the deep end ... Fred Astaire ... watch out ... here I come!'

'Yippee.' said Eileen 'Can I watch?'

Ciara went into the garden, bent down to smell a rose and the nectar reminded her of her own childhood when she'd danced in the garden with her mother.

* * *

Valerie asked Jenny if she could meet her in Bewleys after one of her lectures.

She came in wearing one of her mottled black hats, and an orange feather sticking out. She purchased a pot of Darjeeling tea and brought it to the table, pulled up a chair, poured the lime tea and stirred in spoon after spoon of sugar.

'How was the trip?' Jenny asked.

'The usual ... bomb scare ... the line closed outside Newry. Anyway I'm here. God, the queue, it's getting longer all the time.'

She glanced back. Jenny sipped at her coffee, waiting for the moment to ask her friend what was pre-occupying her but Valerie continued.

'How's Brian?'

Jenny pulled on her cigarette.

'Since when were ye so interested?'

Valerie put the spoon carefully onto the saucer.

'Jenny.' she said with a little authority. 'I know you, do you love him?'

Jenny was taken aback, surprised by her insistence and said:

'Since when have ye been interested?'

'Listen, Jenny, do you really love him?'

She didn't answer.

Valerie annoyed at her silence, threw her spoon onto the table.

'I think he's a jerk.'

Jenny didn't respond. She was surprised by the vindictiveness of her friend.

'Val, ye don't understand, of course I love him, how can

ye say that?'

'Look, he's married. You're making a big mistake!'

Jenny looked hard at her friend, she'd been expecting this lecture for some time.

'Listen Val, we better get one wee thing straight, how many brothers and sisters have yeu?'

'Two.'

'Well, yer father loves yeu doesn't he?'

'Yes of course.'

'Well does he love yer brothers more or less than yeu?'

Valerie sipped some tea.

'The same, I suppose.'

'Well,' said Jenny 'Brian has children and he also has a wife and he loves me the same as them, I know I'm fourth on his list but I know he loves me, ye know.'

Valerie unable to say anything finished her tea. After an uncomfortable silence she looked into her friend's face.

'Jesus, you twist everything around. How could you? How could you do this to yourself?'

'I've told ye.'

'But how could you? Don't you understand? He's using you.'

'Stop tryin' to hurt me. I love this man and that's the way it is, neither yeu or anyone else can ever change that.'

She wondered to herself if she really meant it at all, whether she was defending their passion with words that were hollow. She wondered if Valerie was actually not jealous but caring and said, 'I know the way ye feel Val, I know ye care but I'm happy, happy for the first time in my life and ye have to understand that'.

Valerie shook her head and Jenny continued.

'Ye have to remember Val, he loves me, he's the only man who has made me feel this good about myself, made me really happy, I know what yer sayin' but that's the way it is.'

She glanced at her watch.

'Anyway, I have to go now.'

She stood up. Valerie didn't respond. She sat there silent keeping it in, bending her teaspoon into a V.

* * *

'Do you want a glass?' he asks
'Ye mean, would I like a glass?' Jenny says, correcting him.
'What's the difference?'
'The difference is that 'want' means ye don't actually want to buy me a drink.'
'Well okay, would you like me to buy you a drink, no, on second thoughts, would you like a drink, how's that?' he smiles.
'Ha, ha, very funny, okay, I'll have a pint.'
'At this hour, a glass, surely.'
'No. A pint.'
'Well, I'll have a glass, at least I'm civilised.'
She looks hard at him.
'Civilised ... well, at least, I'm honest.'

*

'I don't like the wig you're wearing today. 'Is it silver or platinum or something?' he asks.
'Yer tryin', but ye can't hurt me.'
'It's a bit ... I dunno'.'
He shrugs his shoulders.
She looks hard at him.
'My father used to say that if ye've nothin' good to say, don't say it, I've told ye that.'
'Yeah well, I'm sure your father said a lot of things.' he says.
'Don't ye dare ever say that again.'
'I'm sorry, it was out of line, your hair today looks, well, fabulous.'

'I hate yer guts.' she says
'I love you.' he says.
'Ye should tell me more often, I have a heart, ye know.'
He says, 'I love you'.
She says, 'I hate your guts.'

*

She breaks down in tears.
'I don't get it.' he says.
She sobs 'Leave me alone, ye always want to know everythin', yet ye don't want to understand.'
She sits up on a plinth that strides one of the pillars under Butt Bridge.
The Dart train passes overhead and she starts fiddling around inside her handbag.
He can't see her eyes, only the tears running across her cheeks.
As though for all the world by hiding them she wouldn't let the world witness her unhappiness.
And she says 'I wish I knew what was happenin' to me, ye know ... I wish I knew what was happenin'.'

*

She stares at him.
'Nobody cares about me the way ye do.'
He says 'You know what they say about the mystery of Love, its need to possess'.
'Yeah' she says 'But make sure ye don't think about that when we're makin' love.'
'What do ye mean?'
She says it slowly. 'Too much possession kills everything. Ha, ha, ha, got ya.'

*

'Brian, do ye know anything about cancer?'
'No.'
'Do ye think it will come back?'
'Jenny, please!'
'Ye know I think it's goin' to come back, I'm so afraid it's goin' to come back.'

*

'I don't like Frank.'
'He likes you.'
'No he doesn't, don't lie to me.'
'He does.'
'Frank stares at me the way men look at mannequins, he wants to hurt everyone.'

*

He asks her.
'Do you dream a lot?'
'Yes I do, when, I've overslept, especially when I've overslept, but it's been so long, I haven't really slept well since the operation.'
'Fantasy, reality, do you ever dream about, well animals?'
He's laughing at her.
'When I sleep, I dream about everythin', I can't dream about animals just like that.'
'You're joking! you're always going on about them.'
'No I can't, if I got sleep, I mean regular, I'm sure it would be different, it would be like Animal Farm, one after the other, I'd be in Heaven.'
She trails away, smiling at this thought. The way her father showed her how to hold them when they had no strength.
He looks through her.

'I love you.' he says.
She looks into his eyes.
'Keep saying that, keep sayin' it, cos' I hate yer guts.'
They kiss big.
Burning through the trouble that's driven each of them towards the other.
She puts her hand behind his head and pulls his ear to her lips.
'I'll dream of this, I'll dream of this.' she says.
The angels sing.
The devil laughs.
And a million lovers dead for a thousand years sigh in their graves.

*

They're in bed.
Both smoking.
The fire smoulders.
He tells her about the Book of Kells.
'You're studying there and you don't know?' he asks.
'Tell me.'
'It's one of the oldest books in the world. Written about 800 AD and it was kept in a monastery in Kells.'
'C'mon, c'mon tell me more.'
She snuggles into him. He continues.
'It was moved around during the Viking raids. It was hidden in vaults, buried and dug up a few times. It's in the Long Room of Trinity, go and see it. There's another two hundred thousand books kept there too.'

*

Jenny says to him 'I keep thinkin' its all my fault, I'm so messed up.'

'I mean I keep thinkin' it's my fault my parents split up.'

*

'Valerie wants to get married'.
'Yeah ... who is he?'
'Me!' she says.
'You're not serious.'
'I am ... I want to start a family. She'd make a great dad.'
He cracks up.

*

She says she doesn't get hang-overs.
He says he gets them bad.
He tells her that sometimes during the day after a session, he walks around doing his work in a suit as though he means business but inside he's dying like a manic depressed clown.
She turns from the sink and smiles at him.
'That's because I'm twenty-two and yer thirty-four.'
He goes quiet.
She comes to him holds his hand and says:
'Well at least ye don't dye yer hair.'
He pulls her down.
'Come here!' he says.
He kisses her lightly on the lips.
She curls beside him.
'Ye know...' she says.
'I was workin' it out the other day, when ye were twenty, I was, well, eight,' she smiles.
There is a long pause.
She continues, 'Maybe yer using me to rebel against yer age. Maybe ye want to crystallise my energy and

keep young yerself, ye know, for ever young,' she says it slowly.

'Ah, c'mon.' he says. 'Don't insult yourself. If you were ninety I'd love you as much but I wouldn't fuck you.'

'Why not?' she asks.

'Because I'd be 102 years old and I'd never get it up!'

*

She screams at him, 'You don't own me.'

* * *

The following Saturday he went to the Blackberry Market in Rathmines. He discovered an antique phonograph, a box of needles and five wooden cartons of 78's, after some haggling he bought the lot and put everything into the back of his car. He saw someone selling fish. He bought a large glass bowl and ten small goldfish in clear plastic bags of water. He left the phonograph in the car and carried the goldfish bowl and the bags of fish up to her flat.

She whooped with delight, and put the glass bowl on the mantelpiece over the fireplace where she could admire them, like her, imprisoned by water.

* * *

She dressed in orange. Orange wig, lipstick, dress, stockings and shoes.

They strolled to Davy Byrnes in Duke Street. The pub had the look of efficiency, men made pinstripe conversation, their mobile phones on the counter.

She ordered a Martini.

He told her he would take her to a restaurant that had just opened. They talked about music, films, 'Monroe, Garbo,

Dean, Sinatra, De Niro' and all the rest.

They were given a table in the centre of the restaurant. All about them there were candles, huge mirrors and waiters weaving past. When she flashed her smile at the man sitting at the table next to them he was knocked out by her power. The wine came over. She told Brian he was opinionated and bombastic.

'Bombastic, what do you mean, bombastic?' he asked.

'Ye know ...' she said leaning into him 'yer always sayin' things like...'

She pitched her voice.

'Some day I'm going to run the biggest bakery in the country, fifty shops, millions, I'm goin' to make millions, I'm this, I'm that, the country's goin' to the dogs, there's no culture of entrepreneurship, ye know.'

Her hands on her hips and her head shaking about the place, doing this act. He got up out of his seat, head to head with her and gave her a line from his favourite film *'Scarface'*, pointing his finger at her nose and in a deep drawl said:

'You don't fuck with me. Don't fuck with me, don't ever fuck with me, ya hear.'

There was silence in the dining room. But some people at a nearby table saw it for what it was and let it go, from the rest only forced smiles and intense stares.

They continued talking as if nothing had happened.

'You remember I was in the market in Rathmines.'

She interrupted him 'They're so dead in here ye'd think ye were at a funeral.'

'Yeah. Anyway, I got something that might interest you, seeing that you're nuts about Mario Lanza and you can't get enough of him ... hold on.'

He folded his napkin on the table and left the restaurant. After some ten minutes he returned with a cardboard box. He placed it on the ground and took out the old phonograph and the 78's. He set it all up on the table, fitted the loudspeaker onto it and fiddled around with a small tin of needles.

Her mouth wide open, her orange hair swishing, guessing what it was all about and jumping about in her seat with anticipation.

He wound it up and swung the arm over, the needle scratched over the black vinyl. He turned a knob and it started to come out with the touch and delicacy that only Lanza knew.

> '*Che bella cosa,*
> *Un giornata al sole,*
> *L'aria e serena,*
> *Dopo la tempesta.*'

The music drifted over the restaurant, the silence testament to the brilliance of the magic voice.

She stood up and went to him. All orange, her squealing and kissing him and her heart thumping with desire and gratitude.

The knowing that this must surely be something she would never experience again and him as mad as herself and as impulsive. Yes, as decent a man as her father was.

'Oh Brian, I could eat ye up, thank ye'.

Brian stole her line 'Don't thank me, thank God you met me.'

* * *

A thunderstorm had picked up over the Atlantic and high winds carried clouds full of salt and rain. He rushed in to her flat with the phonograph and a box of records. As soon as they climbed the stairs he put it on again and through the scratches out came the magnetic voice of the Italian tenor. He opened the windows and listened to the rain orchestrating with the melody.

He found some candles and lit them one by one and put them on a table. She looked into his eyes through the flame of the candles and let the strap on her dress slip over arms.

When he imprinted his kisses on her skin, she felt electricity around her body. She pushed him away and he fell back into an armchair.

'I want to strip for yeu,' she said, touching the edges of her shoulder straps, peeling away the orange gloves and lifting her legs. She saw the effect on him, and removed her dress, revealing an orange basque, orange stockings and the orange garter.

Lanza sang *'Santa Lucia, Santa Lucia, Santa Lucia.'* She rolled her hips about and pushed her breasts out. Brian sat back, smoking his cigar, taking in the aroma of brandy, watching it all in a childlike trance.

Later they lay in bed, him filling her longings with his power and she knew her fate lay in his madness. She moaned through the past, through her life into his life and his sweat, but she knew that the affliction of this terrible desire to have him was only momentarily put to rest by his closeness, that the sun would arrive for her, for them. She knew that the sound of the water was the sound that she wanted to hear. When the rhythm of their lovemaking reached a new plateau she said to him, 'Ye'll never leave me will ye? Ye'll never leave.'

'You're crazy.' he said.

'Yer wild, wild, wild, wild, wild,' she said 'and sometimes I think when the rain stops yeu'll go!'

He began to caress her once again, re-assuring her, touching her nipples with the curve of his hand, tweaking them so that they came out hard, licking them so that the torture of her desire fired up and her wetness ached and her obsession finally and inextricably linked itself to him.

'It feels as if somethin' else is takin' over ... somethin' else' she repeated.

And all that night he was slow, patient, utterly caring and delicate, touching unfathomed depths within her, bringing her time and again to the edge.

The next morning she woke up alone. She sat staring at the spent wax and the sad pool of orange clothes on the floor. She smelt her arms and licked the back of her hands. In her skin she could taste the flavour of his sweat and the scent of his love, she looked at the burnt out candles and she wondered whether it would ever be the same again. Whether the altar of passion on which they had lain would ever be relit to celebrate the ardour of their love.

* * *

The moon was out full and clear. After the rain it was strangely warm. Killiney beach pebbled with grey round pieces of stone.

'Are ye drunk?'

'Probably, yes.'

'Ye'll be cold.'

'I know, who cares.'

'Oh Brian, are ye sure?'

'Here, sit on my jacket.'

He put it over the stones. She sat down and tucked her legs into herself, her head on her knees, she looked at the round and full moon. He stood beside her undressed, knelt and put his mouth over hers.

'I'll be back.'

He walked in and waded out. She saw his shoulders going into the night fading until she could only hear his splashes. He swam strongly, flipping under the water, diving into the belly of dark water. She listened to the wash, sucking pebbles into itself and she wondered whether if it was the moon sucking them into each other.

'Jenny!' he shouted 'I'm here.'

She looked to her left.

'How are ye? Are ye cold? Are ye there? I can barely see ye. I'm so cold lookin' at ye. Please be careful.'

'I'm fine, are you okay?'

He went under again, surfaced and spat out water.

'I can't swim.' she said. 'I wish I could but no one ever brought me in the water, Brian will ye teach me?'

A swell moved under him and he was pulled by the current

but his powerful even strokes took him back towards the shore.

'Are ye there, are ye there? I can't see ye, please, please don't go too far.'

'I'm here, don't worry. I love the water, I've always loved it.'

'I love the beach.' she answered relieved. 'I love the feelin' of land under me. When I was young my father, he'd bring me to Portrush, I've always wanted to go back, ye know the beach. Can ye hear me? Brian, can ye hear me?'

The moon watched.

The sea breathed as each wave curled into her feet.

They didn't talk yet they said even more. Silent talk. The kind you have between yourself and someone close to you who's dying. You hold their hand and it's all there. Silent talk. The kind you have in a quiet place and you think it might be St. Joseph or one of the saints you haven't heard about.

Silent talk, the kind you have when your baby's being born and you feel something around you, between you, your woman, your child, that kind, you know the way it can be.

In the moonlight, on the beach over the sea.

Everything.

Silent talk.

The beat.

* * *

That same night Ciara pulled her pearl necklace from her jewellery box, wrapped it in newspaper and flushed it out to sea, out from her and he never knew and he would never find out and she thought back to the night of the Trinity Ball and the way she didn't want to wear them.

* * *

He called by late one afternoon and washed some mussels in the kitchen sink.

'I'm used to getting this done for me, you know.'

Jenny sat at the table.

'Well I'm not cookin' for ye ... every time you show up here, don't expect me to cook for you anyway. It's yer turn.'

He looked at her.

'Listen, I'm not making an issue of this.'

He thought about how he'd never cooked a meal for his wife and that now the roles had reversed.

She played with the cutlery and toyed with a wine glass, running her nail around the rim. She moved up close to him, the smell of his breath surprised her. She remembered how he had told her that his wife detested the smell of garlic, instinctively she felt he'd eaten it with someone. No, it couldn't be that or could it? But she knew his smells and her smells on him and that afternoon while they made love she felt sure, behind it all, that he was doing it to give her the feeling he was with her but that behind all the closeness, he'd lost the slowness, the strange delicacy he always had when it meant something.

When they finished he stared beyond her. Even the way he touched at the fabric of the sheets, pre-occupied, running his fingers across the stitching on the pillow, distracted by something else outside them, cold. She was sure. Sure that his moves had been changed by something, someone, maybe it was in that moment she discovered a truth. At that very moment, her own insecurity about everything and that maybe this was the beginning of some form of possessiveness.

Later that afternoon, he made a turf fire and put candles into it letting the wax light it up. She sat at the table drinking black coffee. There were pineapples all over the flat. He sat down and peeled the shell of the fruit away from its flesh.

'Sometimes I think you're trying to make me into something I'm not,' she said 'Sometimes I think ye want me to be yer slave and only yer slave.'

'What?'

'I'm yer mistress but I want some respect.'

And after a while, 'Ye've been with somebody, haven't ye?'

'Don't be crazy.'

'Do ye think I'm that naive. Ye've been with someone haven't ye, haven't ye, haven't ye? I can smell it from yeu!'

'Don't be ridiculous.'

'Ye better not.'

She stared hard into his face, to invoke truth, let it go and said, 'I'm sorry, I'd hate to feel, well ye know ... someone else that's all.'

'Listen Jenny, it might come as a surprise, I've enough trouble trying to keep this together, besides I hate your guts.'

She laughed but she wasn't sure.

* * *

Ciara opened her bag and spilled out the contents on the table, she shouted to him 'This is my life.'

Jenny opened her bag, put everything over the table and said: 'Ye know, I'm sick of possessions, I'm sick of all this!'

* * *

JENNY'S SHOPPING LIST
Make up: Cover Girl
Lipstick
Eyeliner
Mark Quant eyeshadow
Screen face, Fardel
Iridescent powder
Mary Quant nail polish, blue
Toothpaste
Pearl drops
Moisturiser

CIARA'S SHOPPING LIST
Washing powder
Nappies, disposable
Bread
Fruit
Fish fingers
Beans
Toilet paper
Chicken
Pizzas, three medium
Butter

Cotton Wool
Toilet Paper
Wine, red
Cartons of orange juice
Cigarettes
Box of tissues

Yoghurts
Cheddar cheese
Flour
Oat Flakes
Cereal
Milk
Soup-packet

SOME CONTENTS OF
JENNY'S HANDBAG
Night-club passes
A loose contraceptive
Raffle ticket
Cigarettes
Lighter
Contraceptives
Make-up
Pencil parer
25p

SOME CONTENTS OF
CIARA'S HANDBAG
Supermarket Receipts
Blood Donor card
Child Allowance Book
Sweet Papers
Calendar
Keys
Earrings
Loose change
VISA card

* * *

They put the children to bed. Their daughter Eileen had finished writing her story and they were all looking forward to it. The two children brushed their teeth, tucked themselves up and Brian asked:

'Ciara, where's the story have you got it?'

'Mummy has it, Mummy has it.'

'Have you kids said your prayers yet?' Brian asked.

'We were waiting for Mummy.'

'Okay, out you get.'

Ciara walked in and they all knelt around the bed.

'Oh angel of God my guardian dear,
To whom God's love commits me here,
Ever this night
Be at my side,

To light and guard,
To rule and guide.
Amen.

'Michael you can't make faces when your talking to Jesus,' Ciara said.

Michael looked at her, 'I want to talk to Jesus by myself ... not with everybody else.'

'Okay Michael, we'll stop and you can talk by yourself,' she said.

There was silence and Michael said in a soft voice 'Hello Jesus'.

After a moment he turned to Ciara 'See!' he said raising his hands 'There's nobody there!'

Brian buried his head.

Ciara continued with the prayers.

'There are four corners around my bed,
There are four angels around my head,
St Mathew, St Mark, St Luke, St John,
God bless the bed that I lie on.
Amen'

'Right, Michael into bed and I'll read you Eileen's story,' Brian said.

Michael dived in, blessed himself the wrong way round, the right way and again the wrong way. Eileen blessed herself and said, 'Daddy there's some words I haven't put in, but you'll know them. Will you read it slowly?'

'Don't worry sweetheart, we'll know.' He sat on the end of his son's bed.

'Once upon a time there lived a little elf. Her name was Dotty. Dotty didn't live in a usual tiny elfy house. She lived in a human house but it took her six hours to climb the stairs. The really strange thing about her was that it took her only two minutes to go down the same stairs. Everybody thought that this was magic but it wasn't, it was a secret.'

He stopped. Michael's eyes were wide open.

'So one day when a boy in Dotty's class called Elfy got up he dressed and went straight to Dotty's class. He took out a very big ladder and put it up to Dotty's bedroom window. He was amazed by what he saw. He saw Dotty drinking a magic potion. It said on the label, "This is a potion for slow people," and on the other side it said, "Drink one dose and then click your fingers and you will be able to run really fast, so much so that you won't be able to see a single thing". Elfy looked to see if Dotty was in her room but she wasn't there. So then Elfy looked down the road and there was Dotty going to school really fast. Elfy said to himself "maybe if I drink that magic potion, I might be able to run as fast as Dotty!" So he sneaked into Dotty's room and drank a dose of it and then clicked his fingers and suddenly he was off in a second, two minutes later he was in school. But as Elfy was sitting in school he couldn't help himself. He had to tell everybody about the magic potion in Dotty's bedroom. Then all the people in their school started to drink the magic potion. Everybody started to get faster and faster and faster. So when Dotty discovered that everyone was exactly the same as her she said to herself, "I was always different from the others now I'm the same so I'm going to stop taking the magic potion and I'll be different again." They never saw Dotty again, that is, with the magic potion in her hands. Dotty was really happy because she knew she could make the potion and when they ran out of the potion she could be different again even though she knew that she wouldn't be able to go outside the house and show the world. So Dotty built a new house for herself in really quick time and it only took her two seconds to get up and down the staircase.'

During the tale, Ciara watched her husband closer than she had ever done before, his mouth, the lines across his forehead.

She looked into his eyes for the lies in them and found only the reflected disquiet of her own unease.

'Eileen' he said 'That's really good, that is the best story I've ever heard. Did you really write that all on your own?'

'Yep, all on my own.'

'Well I think that's brilliant.'

He kissed both of them and switched out the light.

'Night, night everybody sleep tight.'

The reply came 'and don't let the bedbugs bite.'

But Ciara went to bed that night unsure, sleeping away from him in silence, alone, listening to the ticking of her watch against the heat of her ear and thinking to herself that maybe Brian had found a potion, a drug that was taking him from her.

* * *

He was in Jenny's flat.

'What are the wigs made from?'

She walked out of the shower with a cap and wrapped in a red towel.

'What are ye lookin at?'

'What are your wigs made from?'

'Mono-fibre, ye know.'

'What's that!'

'Well all I know is that it's stronger than acrylic and nylon or hair, ye know, ordinary hair and ye don't get split-ends.'

'They look so real.'

He touched them. She thought how innocent he was, how she'd never have gone for him if he hadn't been that way.

'They're supposed to.'

'I prefer the blonde one, the platinum is weird, how do they get those hairs curled?'

She laughed, drying herself.

'They're permed, all the wigs are permed, that's what it's called Brian. Permed.' She mouthed the word slowly and kissed him.

She kissed him again.

She dried her hair, standing naked, her wet skin glistening. He looked at her.

'Listen I don't want to worry you but I had a call from your mother's boyfriend, what's his name?'

'What! Who rang? Who did ye say?'

She stared at him rigid with fright.

'Wallace. Yeah, his name was Wallace.'

She grabbed a chair and stared at him.

'Wallace rang!'

'Yeah that's what I said. He said his name was Wallace.'

'How did he get yer number? I mean, Jesus!'

'You tell me, I'm ex-directory.'

She walked over to the window overlooking the traders.

'Jesus, Wallace rang, what the hell did he say?'

He took a cigar from his top pocket and lit it. He acted like it meant nothing.

'He threatened ye, didn't he?' she asked.

He blew smoke.

'Yeah, to put it mildly.'

'Jesus, I told ye, they always find out ... always, always.'

She walked around, looking through the pockets of her coat for a cigarette.

'Listen!' he told her 'it doesn't make any difference ... you should give those things a miss.'

'Brian, ye can be so dangerous, ye know. Fools only go ...' she said ignoring his advice.

She found a packet of cigarettes and took one out, her hand shaking.

'I'm so afraid.' she said lighting it.

He laughed.

'Bollocks, you think too much about it.'

'I know him, he's killed people, it means nothin' to him. He doesn't have any fear in him.'

Brian drew on his cigar.

'How many people has he killed?'

'Jesus, I don't know how many, he doesn't exactly come and tell me when he's bumped someone off does he, I mean, it would be like askin' ye how many lovers ye've had.'

'I'd tell you.' he said.

'Like hell ye would, ye'd tell me a lie, yer great at hidin' yer past.'

'Jenny, I don't lie.'

'Well, tell me what Wallace said?'

He watched the traders below.

'He told me to lay off in so many words, but he kept saying, 'what are you?' or something like that.'

'What about ye?' she looked up at him.

'That's it, that's the one, what about ye, that's it, does he say that all the time or is he trying to sound heavy?'

What else? Tell me.' she asked.

'Nothing,' he said, blowing out smoke and continued.

'Listen, this guy doesn't worry me, you make him out to be some kind of all-powerful fuckin' gangster.'

She moved to him, really serious.

He turned around to face her.

'Brian, I'm afraid, I'm afraid,' she said and looked up at him. He held her tight to him.

'I don't run from anyone, do you hear me?'

'Brian believe me, ye don't want to start actin' big with him, he'd break ye in two pieces ... for fun.'

They both stared out the window. Jenny in her underwear, her left hand clutching her cigarette, her right hand in her mouth.

* * *

'Why didn't ye ring me?' she asked.

'I couldn't, I can't.'

'Why didn't ye use a phone box, anything, get one of those card phones, ye should have rung.'

He looked through her.

'You're beginning to sound like my wife.'

She bit her lip, keeping it all in and he continued:

'Somedays I can't ring you, I've got a business, twenty employees, a new bank manager who's the most negative bastard I've ever met, people who won't pay their bills, a son with a toothache.'

She stared at him.

Ye've got to ring, I get lonely.'

'Lonely, lonely, Jenny everyone is lonely, we can't be together all the time, you know that.'

'Ye don't understand. Nobody understands me. I'm so scared they'll come up to Dublin.'

'Listen Jenny ... it was a warning that's all.'

'I need more time from ye. Don't ye understand ... if ye can't give it to me, go, get out of here!'

She stood up and went into the kitchen.

'Please!'

He was surprised.

'If that's what you want.'

'Leave me alone.'

When he left she opened a press door, took out a mug put in a spoon of coffee and stared at another spider trying to weave its trap against the corner of the kitchen window.

She started to cry, the frustration pouring out, into the sink.

She saw a butterfly trapped in the spider's web, she thought that the final days of summer were like that butterfly waiting to die, its wings stiff and tired. She hoped that the rain would never cease, would never leave her, would always follow her around.

* * *

The traders sold the last punnets of strawberries and for the first time that summer, the sun came out. He rang her and said that they should spend more time together, that they would cut through the distance imposed on them by his absence, that the very act of making love would erase her tension. He would spend time away from work, wait for her until she returned from the library.

She found herself caught in the trap of her imagination, so that during the day while she sat at her desk in the library, she could think of nothing more important than this man, than the touch of his fingers running across the swell of her breasts.

They closed the shutters to the heat and light and during that shortest of weeks he stripped away all her inhibitions, until at the moment of each surrender she became true to herself, unlocking passions that had been hibernating within her and yet strangely, she never orgasmed, never felt the full release of it, as though the closer she got to him, the more remote it became.

She woke one morning and his lips were over hers. It felt for a moment that she was going into his mouth, his throat, his soul.

She woke another morning and he was inside her and she was defenceless in submission.

On the Thursday afternoon of that warm week, he gave an operatic rendition which he had prepared, using the Italian words in the dictionary as his lyrics.

'*Amor, casa, stupendo, miasma, mangiare, difficolta.*'

He carried cards which he raised as he sang so that she could see the words.

'You are poison.'

And:

'Demon.'

And:

'I will die for you.'

And:

'Save me.'

Finally, he pulled out a plastic sword and pretended to stab himself as he sang and collapsed onto the floor. Jenny cried tears of laughter and applauded in uncontained glee, clapping until the ripples of her applause cascaded into the deep caverns of her memories of that week but sometime afterwards she found the cards with those words and wondered about their significance.

Afterwards for days, she goaded him with:

'My little Pavarotti, *L'uomo con la voce ducelli.*'

The man with the voice of the birds.

And when the week finished she wanted him more. But it never really ended. Every day she carried it around with her, like the moon over Killiney beach and the memory of those days and nights returned with their intensity to bring her happiness, the way the rhythm of his lovemaking touched the plateau of her own fulfilment, the union of their kiss met the tremors of her heart, ardour whirling into the vortex of rapture and rapture and rapture. Her life, her breath, her body his to dominate, abuse, nurture, care for, feed and starve and by her endless submission urging his desire, the desire that stoked the sweetest ecstasy.

A week later she tried to masturbate, driven to it by the involuntary frenzy within herself fantasising about his movements on top of her and in her, the picture of his cock brushing against her clitoris, her own fingers becoming his cock, circling around the wetness, his tongue flicking her nipples. Even then she never orgasmed, it was as though the rain would never see her hunger satisfied, leaving her expectant, craving and wanting him even more and for days she walked around Dublin thinking solely of her need to be possessed.

* * *

He drove the van to the Dublin Mountains easing it around the hills, with the wind blowing across, swaying it about. They reached a pig farm and slid the side door of the van open and emptied out the containers. The pigs went delirious, snorting, slurping with their mouths chomping and rolling.

They took the van to Johnny Fox's, a pub high in the Dublin mountains. Brian wound down the window.

Frank started: 'Who wants to be tied down when you see all this freedom around you?'

'Frank, without them what's the point?' he replied.

'Look it's like this, if you get emotionally attached they're treacherous and that's what you're doing.'

'What are you saying?'

'Look Brian, I never tell them I love them, so I starve them of that, it makes them want to prove themselves to you, sometimes I say to them, look you have to make me dependent on you, you understand what I'm saying, you have to make me dependent on you.'

Frank was pointing his finger at the windscreen.

'Here we go,' Brian said.

'No I'm serious. Don't give them any power, always control them, look it's like this, sometimes when I want to get control I screw them but I don't, you know, finish, right, half way through I get up, light a cigarette and get dressed, say I want to get some work done or coffee or do something totally irrelevant. You see, Brian, they want to control you through their fanny, you understand it's so simple for them. Women know they control you through sex, so you've got to have the strength to turn the tables around.'

Brian laughed and later, in Johnny Fox's with its turf fires and Liscannor stone, they drank dark creamy stout and listened to traditional Irish music.

'Maybe I've gone too far,' Brian said.

'Of course you have, I tell you, no woman will ever give you what she wouldn't give somebody else.'

'Crap Frank. That's utter crap. That's true about anyone.'

Frank continued.

'You've got to control them, once they know they're in control you're gone, look it's like this, four years ago I met a girl, beautiful, Karen, she could have been a model.'

Brian laughed.

'Don't tell me you drugged her with your charm, you gave her half a fuck and she never left you alone.'

Frank got serious.

'Believe me, I'm showing you the way.'

He wiped the Guinness from his lips.

'Anyway this girl, she came back to my place and she's undressing, wearing only black knickers, she goes over to the stereo and puts on a Simply Red tape. Now I know, 'a' that she's never listened to Simply Red before and, 'b' she's never worn black knickers, it's obvious, she's seeing someone else, he's changing her, showing her a different environment, so she comes to the bed and I ask her, "Are you playing the numbers game?" '

'What do you mean,' Brian interrupted.

'I mean is she sleeping around, you know the numbers game? And that was it, goodbye, and do you know for four years I never heard from her. So there she is in outer space and after four years she rings, you see Brian the signal is still going, and the reason she rings is because I wouldn't let her get control, but I said, look too much water's gone under the bridge, okay. I'm sorry, this isn't the movies, good-bye. The parachute.'

They finished and returned to the van. The wind whipped up and they wound down the gorse-covered hills back into Tallaght.

'Listen', Frank continued, 'all women are coded, you have to break the code, they're all coded, look I'll give you an example, there's a group of women sitting together in a pub right, they're having their chit-chat talking about the price of eggs and who's going to get their hair done and all the usual shit. Right, well you go over to the best looking of them, the one who's really made the effort and say really quiet into her ear, "I don't think you're as good looking as you think you are", always gets a reaction, but what you're doing is you're breaking her code, that's what you're doing, she's putting on that make-up for any man, remember, no woman will give you what she wouldn't give somebody else. You've got to control them and you're not. She's got you, that girl Jenny!'

'Shut up.' Brian said.

'It's true.'

'Bollocks!'

'I'll tell you one thing. That girl Jenny and you. You and the cheque book. You'll end up having a cheque-book relationship and wrecking our business. I'm telling you. Spread yourself around, Brian, it's cheaper. You see, fuck all this Jenny stuff, she'll wreck your marriage Brian, I'm telling you, she's got you. She's high maintenance and she'll destroy you.'

* * *

There were twelve people in the dance class. They stood behind the teacher, a small man who wore navy blue pants and his wife with a loose sequinned top and black skirt.

'Now I want you to start by watching me closely, watch my feet, this is the Cha-Cha,' the teacher said.

He looked at his partner. She smiled and with a little shyness raised her eyes to heaven. Her hair was perfect.

'Now as I was saying the Cha-Cha comprises four basic moves. The New Yorker, the Cuban Break, the Fan and of course the Alemana .'

'First , I want you to watch Betty and myself, I'll put the music on.'

He pressed one of the buttons on the portable stereo and walked back into the centre of the floor. He took his wife, pointed to his nose as though he was trying to recall the steps and waited to meet the music slowly. The two of them reeled into dance, stepping into each other, holding elbows and spiralling into a swing of hips and shoulders as they passed and repassed each other.

After a time he returned to his students. They were entranced. 'From the hips, no movement, you can master any step once your legs become flexible, that's the key', he said.

Brian concentrated. Ciara practised.

'Okay, let's start again with the steps. The ones I'm going to teach you first are complicated. But I don't want you worrying about that because when you master these you can master any variations.'

He went over to the stereo, rewound the tape and switched it on.

'Now watch, watch my feet.'

He put his left foot forward and brought it back.

'Now side to side and then right foot up and side to side, now altogether, follow me, very good, keep doing it, okay, girls concentrate on your steps, that's it side to side, very good, oh yes, you see, stop everyone.'

He walked over to the stereo and stopped it.

'Look, it's like driving a car. In the beginning you think oh my God how can I let this pedal out and put that pedal back in at the same time and let off the hand brake and all the rest of it and after six months you're lighting cigarettes and chatting about the weather and all the time you're changing gears and putting on the brakes and you're not conscious of it at all. So what I'm saying is, don't be afraid, keep repeating what you're doing now and it will all sort itself out, organise yourselves, right, come on left foot up, back, side to side, very good.'

He switched on the music. Brian started on the wrong foot, tripping and collapsed into Ciara's arms. Not once, three times. The teacher stopped and shook his head.

Thursdays, Mondays. Sometimes the classes got larger, sometimes smaller since those with little patience or through boredom left, but Brian and Ciara persisted and they improved. The tango, the slow step, the quick step, the cha-cha, the waltz, the fox-trot, the jive and the samba. They practised at home in their kitchen until they discovered through the dances that they had created a bond ,the bond of the dance.

In their minds they were Miguel and Ramona.

Was it the freshness of the moves? Or was it the appetite to conquer this new art form that enthralled them? Was it the exhaustion they felt after each session? Or was it the plain truth that they were still attracted to each other? Was it the simplicity of these very steps danced around the world on every continent in exactly the same way? Or was it the feeling of victory that encompassed them when they knew they were moving well? Together.

During this time Ciara seemed to have become even smoother, softer, more gentle as though the dancing itself had re-established her femininity. Some evenings when she went to her classes she wore exotic perfumes, knowing that it was exciting him and he led her around the floor twisting and turning, whirling and pivoting through steps aroused by the pulse of music and the excitement of that discipline. For three weeks they charged into it, a couple possessed by performance.

* * *

He gave Ciara a lift to Blackrock to visit her parents. They passed by Sandymount Strand. Gulls hovered like kites high up on the wind. It was one of those mornings that if you looked out across the sand you'd wonder how the ships could actually sail into Dublin harbour because the tide was way out as far as the eye could see, as though Howth on the far side of Dublin Bay was a giant hill growing out of the sand. Brian could see the ripples of the sand and the diggers going for lug worms and great heaps of dark soil.

'Sometimes when you move Brian, after the second turn on the Cha-Cha, you don't step side to side.'

'Of course I do, I always step side to side. Listen, I'm finding it difficult enough.'

'No you don't, that's what he said last night, you're lazy on that second step and because you don't move your feet properly you're trying to compensate on the side step, I mean overcompensate.'

'That's because you don't come back far enough on the turn and then you move away too quickly.' he replied.

'No way, you're the one at fault.'

'Hold on a minute.' he said and manoeuvred the car into the car park, they drove in, stopped and he said:

'When you rotate your hips at the turn, you come in too far that's why I have to step back and that leaves me short.'

'I don't come in too far, that's ridiculous, I'm always right, Betty said I was the best mover in the class.'

'Okay, look I'm not denying that, I'm only saying, look get out of the car.'

'What here?'

'Yeah.'

She opened the door.

'Here!' she repeated.

'Hold on, I've got the old record player in the boot.'

He pulled out the antique phonograph and rested it on the ground.

'Not here!' A big smile on her face. 'At this hour?'

'Why not?' he asked, burrowing in the box 'Here we are.' he said holding up a record.

'Moonlight Serenade, remember the Ball.'

He wound it up.

'Oh shit.' he exclaimed 'I forgot the speaker.'

He hauled out the dome from the boot and attached it, swung the needle and placed it delicately on the record. The sound of Glen Miller's orchestra poured over the car park and he held her and she felt the old Brian in her arms, the impulsive mad Brian, her husband, mad for her and smelt the fervour from his skin, saw the look of desire in his eyes and she forgot about the pearls and fell for him all over again.

She never visited her parents instead they drove to the Dublin mountains, made love in the car and drank a hundred hot whiskies in the Blue Light.

* * *

Valerie and Jenny sat on the top floor in the Powerscourt Centre, someone played a piano below them. Valerie wore a black dress, black top and a walkman around her neck, they drank coffee.

'Well, how would it make you feel if you saw him with his wife?'

Jenny said nothing. Valerie lit a cigarette.

'He's using you, look at him, he doesn't know the meaning of the word faithful.'

Jenny was quiet, watching the pianist run his fingers across the keys.

'Ye've no right to talk about him like that.' she said loudly 'besides, I don't like routine.'

'There's no need to shout, Jen.'

'I'm not, I'm just tellin' ye I don't like routine relationships and I wish ye'd stop goin' on and on, why can't ye let us be, anyway, he doesn't think about it being a big permanent thing, he's different, it's like sometimes I'm dealin' with a child, he's like me, it's all impulsive and honest.'

Valerie tried to restrain laughter.

'It's pathetic, you're pathetic, he's pathetic, the whole fucking thing is pathetic,' she spelled it out loudly.

'I'm goin'.' Jenny stood up.

'No don't, I'm sorry.'

She sucked on her cigarette. After a time Valerie asked, 'Is he good? You know?'

'Mind yer own business.'

Jenny lit up. She blew a smoke ring and watched it circle, hover and break into wisps over her coffee. She understood in that moment that she would always be on the outside of everything.

'He knows all the tricks.'

'I bet he can't use his tongue like me.' Valerie said.

'Stop will ye. Ye know it's the first time in my life that I've felt wanted, protected, loved, secure.'

'Secure, ha, Jen, you're the most insecure person I know, come off it, Jesus, have you forgotten he's married.'

'Exactly.'

'I don't understand you, he might be good for you, but you'll never keep him.'

Jenny sipped her coffee and stared over the balcony down at the shoppers, their bags, their pre-occupation with acquisition. She thought to herself, how miserable they all looked, she turned.

Ye know Val, ye know something, I'd love to see him do well, really well, be really successful.'

'He doesn't deserve it and he doesn't deserve you. You only fancy him because he breaks the rules, why can't you face up to the truth.'

Jenny raised her eye-brows and smiled.

'Val, ye know what he said the other day, he said he didn't care about ye, he knew what ye were up to, I was goadin' him on and he said ... he said it was all incest, you and me, ye know, an Ulster Protestant and you being English and all that.'

'He's afraid of me isn't he, isn't he?' Valerie demanded.

'Valerie I'm tired I don't want a fight.'

Jenny hesitated and leaned forward.

'Ye know I wish, just one wish, one wee wish, that it could go on forever, I dunno, he makes me happy.'

'You're rattling my cage, Jen.'

'No I'm serious, at first I wasn't sure whether it would last, but just the last wee while it's been like, well like a dream, give us one of yer cigarettes will ye?'

'God you're such a beggar, do you ever buy anything?'

'Val don't start, ye owe me ten pounds, remember?'

Valerie got serious.

'Do you love him or do you like the idea of being 'in love'?'

'What do ye mean?'

'I know you Jen and I know you want emotional security,

because of your mum leaving for that guy Wallace.'

'Ye think so, do ye really think so?'

'Children from broken marriages are like that, it's always been the way, they crave affection, they end up possessing things, people, they can't let go, let go of anything. I can't make it any clearer than that.'

'Well, Val, I don't care what ye have to say about him, he's in here.'

She hammered her chest, beating it like a monkey.

'And that's all that matters, right inside, Val, right inside.'

She flicked her hair, Valerie took a final drag from her cigarette and stubbed it out as two shoppers sat down at a table behind them.

'He's in me Val, I'm sorry but that's the way it is, ye know.'

Valerie stood up.

'I've got to go. I'm not listening to this anymore.'

Jenny looked into her friend's face, unsure whether she'd hurt her by saying the things she believed.

Valerie said 'I'll call you, maybe we'll go to that night-club, the new one.'

'Yeah great, call to the flat, some night, call me when ye come up to Dublin again.'

'Pathetic Jen, I mean it.'

But Jenny turned away.

* * *

Brian and Jenny and were outside a restaurant in Castle Market Street in the fashion industry area and sat on plastic chairs, the sunlight fell over them and into their drinks.

'I love that Muddy Water's line "I've got to drink me some champagne, smoke some reefer and I hope some school boy starts a fight".' he said.

'Forget reefers, give me E any day.' she said.

Two glasses of wine arrived.

'Don't ever do drugs in front of me', he said.

'Oh touchy,' she said.

'No, I'm serious, if you do, we're finished.'

'Brian, I'm only messin', ye know.'

'You'd better be.' He said, looking into her unsure about it.

A trolley passed laden with hangers, clothes and plastic bags. A model posed in front of them, doing a photo shoot. Two photographers dressed in black snapped her from different angles getting the girl to stare into the camera. She wore a light cream suit and matching shoes. He looked at Jenny.

'I don't mean to be rude, but how do you get your money?'

She played with her lighter surprised by the question.

'Well, my mother sends a wee allowance, my father left it to me, I mean enough for me to get through college, on condition, ye know the usual, study, pass my exams, I told ye all that stuff...'

She paused and dragged on her cigarette.

'Ye know, she, well I think she wants to live through me or somethin'.'

He became distracted by the model pouting into the camera.

'I'd love to get plastic surgery, I'd love to get my boobs done, ye know, small,' she said.

'You're kidding.' he said raising his eyebrows but she put her hands on her breasts and pushed them down.

'Don't be ridiculous.'

'I'd love to get my teeth capped actually, and a wee bit out of my nose as well, it's too big.'

He wasn't listening.

'I'd love to get boobs that really sit flat, sort of neat like hers.' she said annoyed.

He listened to the cameras whirring, watching the model pout and charm the lenses and he turned to her.

'This is stupid, you're fine, you're insecure that's all.'

But he stared out past her. Someone passed with a bag full

of clothes and plastic hangers. Jenny's teeth were clenched, in a moment she got up, purred at the girl and walked across the street, swivelling her hips for all she was worth, her hands up around her face and her hair, jerking her head around, posing like she'd been at it for years.

Sure enough the photographers started to snap away at her as they went in close and backed off, full of enthusiasm for this new find. The elder of the two exclaimed excitedly, 'Yes, yes, yes, yes.'

The model, isolated, had her hands on her hips, indignant. Brian was bent double with laughter, he started to clap, huge hands coming together announcing his pride. She came to him, sat down, sipped some wine.

'Don't ye ever look at another woman when yer with me.'

'I love you.' he said.

'I hate yer guts.' she replied but she knew inside that her courage had worked something.

When she kissed him that night she thought how simple and honest it all was, that he was as basic and straight as the animals she loved, that with his sweat he even smelt like them, that he was just a creature of the world and she was a Goddess, controlling him, that the performances she put on would always pull him away from himself, attract him into her like an insect into the stamen of a flower and she would smother him with the nectar of her passion.

* * *

They walked around the duck pond in St. Stephen's Green.

'I've missed my period.'

There was a pause.

'You sure?'

'It's the fourteenth, isn't it?'

'I made a lodgement this morning, yeah it is.'

'Yer always good on time, bad on dates. I'm serious Brian, I'm late.'

Kissing the Orange

'Late!'

'Well, yesterday was the thirteenth.'

She started to count back days on her fingers, after a few moments she said, 'I'm four days over.'

They stopped walking and stood on a small bridge overlooking the pond and watched ducks paddling past bread crusts on the silt water.

'Hold on a minute. I know this stuff', wait, how long between each period.'

'Ah Brian, c'mon ... between twenty-seven and thirty-two days, I thought ye would have done biology.'

'Thirty-two, right, well now let's work it back.'

'There's no point, I'm late, I know it, ye know.'

'Stop being so paranoid, work it back so that you know absolutely when you finished your last one.'

'Exactly, well I dunno, I think it was, the eighth of last month, I have it in a diary, but it could have been later and that was a week-end and I missed a couple of my pills.'

She trailed off as he looked at her:

'Jesus, what the hell!' and asked, 'You're saying you could be pregnant?'

'Well I'm late, that's all.'

'Hold on, start working it out, hold on I have a pen.'

He fiddled around inside his pockets, eventually finding a biro, pulled out a napkin and began to write numbers down.

'Today is the fourteenth, yesterday is the thirteenth, the twelfth was Tuesday, Monday the eleventh, Sunday the tenth, Saturday the ninth, right that's it twenty-eight days, that was a Wednesday, now Jenny.'

He looked up.

'Was Thursday the day you finished?'

'I don't know, anyway ye take it from when they started, do ye know anythin' about women?'

She wondered when she had said this if he would deflect himself away from the responsibility, if he would leave her in the isolation of motherhood, if the relationship meant nothing to him, if the pond would lift up and swallow her into its filthy embryo.

'Well do you remember any details about that week?' he asked.

'God Brian, I don't know, four weeks ago, I don't remember, I'm sure they're late, well, maybe let's wait a couple of days.'

'Okay, but can't you take one of those tests.'

'Jesus I hate those things, just leave it.'

'Come on we'll walk on, my God, are you sure?'

'Well don't start again, I told ye I don't know.'

They walked for a while and she suddenly felt glad that she was with him, counting the days off and inside she was laughing at it, at the way he'd taken it, reassured by his concern.

He looked at her his eyes full of disquiet.

'Yes I'm sure I'm late.' she said.

'Look let's us work it all out again backwards.'

She laughed.

'Yer funny when ye get worried like this, ye'd swear the whole world was goin' to come in.'

He looked rigidly at her with the pen in his hand, scribbling on the back of her cigarette box.

'Today is the fourteenth, hold on wait, there's thirty-one days in July, hold on now, there's one day and say you actually finished on the Thursday or say even the Friday, well there's two days, Jenny are you listening?'

She raised her eyes and looked at the grey clouds gathering.

* * *

The following afternoon her period started. It began to rain. Big drops of water that made the steam rise from the ground and suffocate the heat. Rain that filled ponds, lakes, drains and gutters. Rain that cooled the little heat there was that summer. It was the rain that changed everything, washing away the sweat, the dirt and the shit from the drains and the happiness on peoples faces.

They drank wine but after they'd made love the tension returned. She felt the sensation of dissatisfaction as though she had been used, had been a target for his physical needs. She'd always needed patience, the patience that comes with real passion and care and when he finished, he got straight up and began to put his shirt on. She felt his strained, almost indifferent eyes and said to him.

'Is yer bed warm when ye go home?'

'Don't give me that line.'

She went for a cigarette.

'Ye know what I mean.'

'Jesus, do you always need re-assurance? I'm having a hard time, I don't have time for this rubbish!'

He started to tie his shoes. She picked up a book that lay beside the bed and threw it, hitting him on the shoulder, she shouted.

'Well when do ye have the fuckin' time?'

She threw a second and a third book. He didn't react.

'C'mon, leave it out, I've got to go home, do some stuff, make a load of calls, anyway, I'm taking Ciara to that new club on Dawson Street.'

She dropped her head.

'Ye mean the Mud Club?'

He looked a little uncomfortable.

'I've been promising her I'd take her there for God knows how long, I mean every day she asks me when am I going to take her out, I mean Jesus, Jenny, fair is fair.'

'But ye told me ye were goin' to take me there, what about me, I always lose out, ye don't give a damn about me.'

In a passion of anger she charged out of bed.

'Ye think ye can come in here and switch me on and off like a machine, well, I'm not a machine and ye can't treat me like one, I'm yer mistress and ye better start treatin' me properly,' she shouted.

'Hold on now, hold on, are you saying that you like the idea of being someone's mistress is that it?'

'Ye know well what I mean, don't try and twist the words around, Brian O'Neill, ye know fuckin' well what I mean. I want to go out this evenin' and I want to go out with yeu.'

'You're behaving like a child.'

She began to flail away at his chest.

'Ye promised me ye'd take me there, ye promised, ye promised.'

'I'm sorry I even mentioned the place, I'm sorry I even mentioned tonight to you, Jesus Jenny, you've got to calm down, you can't lose the head every time you don't get your own way.'

'Well that's it then, ye come in here, ye fuck me, treatin' me like a piece of meat and ye walk out to go and see yer, yer, yer fuckin' wife, and take her to some, some night-club like I'm nothin', like some fuckin' wee tart ye pick up on the streets, well go, get out of here, get out.'

She had her hands on her hips. He made it to the door. She picked up a book and threw it across at him. This time it bounced flat against the fireplace close to the goldfish.

'Jenny come on, will you cool down.'

'Get out of here.' she screamed.

Going down the stairs he heard her shout.'

'Ye selfish bastard, I hate ye.'

Later she thought about it and she couldn't understand why her temper was making its impact so strong on her character, why it had its own momentum, why it came out of her like a rat emerging from a hole in the ground.

* * *

It was a new night-club anyone could go there and watch people stroking their egos. It had a high cavernous roof, mounted strobes, spots and lasers which flicked out and spat white light over the metal dance floor. Speakers were built into bare brick walls above the DJ. This place was in. Jeans, leather and the smell of light white wine dribbling across cool.

Brian was weary, knowing he'd drunk too much and his last three drinks had been three too many, as though he'd been trying to come to terms with the complications he'd created for himself.

Ciara stood with him at the bar in a silver dress made of sequins, shimmering and easy, making any man feel the need, she drew up close to him and kissed him on his cheek

They watched the dance floor.

* * *

Jenny made her entrance, she was with Valerie.

At first he didn't recognise her because she had a huge curled blonde hairpiece that ran down her shoulders and her back. She stuck her tongue out at him.

He picked up the two glasses on the counter and made for the balcony, Ciara followed and a waiter showed them to a table overlooking the floor, where they sat and watched the dancers.

After some time, the DJ started to go into rave.

The floor changed. On came the loose clothes and short dresses. The hair breaking in the white light of the strobes, arms jerking out, some entranced, high on E, others trying to get there. Some of the girls provocative, others unsure. All good with their moves, hips, hips, hips, sway, casual.

Brian's eyes were on the floor watching the lasers flick across and wrap dancers in energy and light.

There in its centre Jenny moved, holding her partner in her sex spell. It was Valerie. They danced in an easy momentum bringing more and more attention to both of them, making the music work with them, swimming inside it like dolphins in a circus of eyes freeing out their arms in front of them touching on illusion.

After a time the fever of the music increased, it's intensity matched by the crazy convulsions with which they threw themselves into abandon. Two spots caught them, enveloping the girls in their white lights. All eyes on them, eyes of this audience for them and only them. Jenny exercised her power like a matador marking out his territory, then the dance floor opened, leaving them centre-stage, hands, fingers, arms around each other, close.

Ciara bored by it all stood up, took Brian's hand and led him towards the exit. She stared over the floor at the girl, unsure about it as though she was trying to recall, and they walked out into the night.

It was still raining.

* * *

Valerie sat on the bed, lit a cigarette and watched Jenny getting into the shower. Through the glass she could see the silhouette of her breasts and her hair running across her back.

She sucked smoke in and stared at the glass, took off her black dress, brought it down from her shoulders and dropped it on the floor. She went over to the shower door and opened it, moved in behind Jenny and touched her face. Jenny was tentative and didn't react.

Valerie took the soap from Jenny's hand and brought the bar around her shoulders, her back, across the nape of her neck, foaming the soft down below the nap of hair. Her fingers held the soap carefully as she smoothed out the underarm and traced over to the side of her breast, lifting it with the soap foaming Jenny's nipples. With the point of her fingernail she pushed into the nipple making it taut and expectant. The breast felt as smooth as glass marble.

Jenny began to yield and slowly slid her bottom and back against Valerie's legs, she felt as weightless as a dream and ready to sink into it, and flow with her own oblivion. The nail of Valerie's finger marked into the breast, forcing little half moans as Jenny gave another push back and forward. The bar of soap slipped out of Valerie's hands and the hot water cascaded down bringing Jenny's hair over her face, her nose, her eyes and Valerie kissed her neck and shoulders, her hands touching the scar on her back then sliding over her hips. Jenny breathing hard turned around with her eyes closed and her lips open and they sucked the kiss, running tongues inside their mouths. They pressed in skin to skin and Valerie's hand dropped down and began to stimulate her, caressing her clitoris. She lowered her head down and kissed Jenny's breast sucking in the nipple, teasing it with her teeth.

She bent down further, her hair wet as she tongued and kissed at the folds of pink skin flicking across her clitoris probing until Jenny's nails dug into her shoulders, until her clitoris was hard and exposed.

'Yes, oh yes, yes, right there, oh yes! Exactly there!' Jenny exclaimed.

The water drowned their lovemaking and only their senses reigned. Valerie lifted her face up.

'No, no, don't stop, don't stop, I don't believe it, oh Jesus, oh my God,' Jenny gasped.

Valerie grabbed her and took her to the side of the bed and they dried off, covering each other in white powder so that they almost looked alike.

Jenny had a hazy picture of Brian and herself covered in flour.

'This is crazy Val, this is crazy.'

'It's not that simple, it's not that simple!' Valerie repeated.

They tongued each other until they came, over and over, and Jenny stoned out of her head with alcohol and jealousy, sucking Valerie and thrusting herself into Valerie's mouth, into the centre of her friend's lust and Valerie repeating into the dawn:

'I've wanted you for a long time Jenny ... a long time.'

* * *

The next evening, Brian was in her flat. He pulled the sheets over him and stared curiously at her, he sensed there was a melancholy about her, a mixture of frustration and resentment. Suddenly she told him.

'I went to bed with someone else!'

'What?' he asked.

'I said I went to bed with someone else, ye know, bed, make love, sex. Do ye want me to spell it out for ye, ye know.'

She trailed off and got a cigarette, lit it and walked over to the bed.

'Look Brian, I went to bed with Val.'

'Valerie!' he questioned.

'Yeah she was great, well, um, great, ye know she was really good, I had my first real orgasm, not one, loads of them.'

'What do you mean, what are you saying, in this bed, our bed, with a lesbian, for fucks sake?'

He pointed at the sheet his face full of shock. She indicated the walkman draped on the chest of drawers.

'Ye see those headphones over there ... she left them behind.'

She blew rings of smoke into his face, satisfied by her revenge.

In one move he got his pants, pulled his shirt over him put his shoes on, buckled his belt and grabbed his jacket.

'Where do ye think ye're goin'?' she shouted at him.

He ran downstairs without even looking back at her and opened the hall door. He walked down the stairs and made for the car, incensed by the depravity of her infidelity and the cool way she'd delivered her admission. As he started the car she was there, running out of the building towards his headlights but as he turned the car around, she grabbed onto the passenger door yanked it open and climbed in. He stopped the car, the engine still running. She screamed at him:

'Ye made me do it, Brian ye made me do it.'

He stared back into her desperate eyes and it came to him that when a dog is cornered it'll go for you, it's teeth shining out from its gums.

'Get out of the car.'

I'm not gettin' out.'

'You fuckin' bitch, you get out of the car.'

He switched the engine off and pushed her.

'You fuckin' bitch, get out.'

He climbed out and went to the passenger side but by the time he was there she had already jumped into the driver's seat. He leaned in and grabbed her.

'Take yer hands off me, don't ye dare touch me,' she screamed.

She hit him across the head.

'Bitch, you fuckin' scum bag, bitch, get out of my car!' he shouted.

He grabbed hold of her clothes but she had her feet up, kicking him like a crazed mule. He dived through her legs, gripped her jumper and with anger the source of his strength dragged her out of the car. He threw her onto the road but she had his hair firmly in her clenched fist.

'You fuckin' bitch!' He roared as he grappled with her, throwing her against the railings outside her building. She pulled hard at his hair but he lifted her up and heaved her over the railings. She landed on empty fruit boxes breaking them into splinters of wood.

Her wig fell off rolling over the pavement.

In her hands were two chunks of his hair. He jumped on top of her and grabbed her chin but without her hair and her eyes full of terror she was a stranger to him.

He picked up her wig, tossed it beyond her and got into his car.

'I didn't realise, I was only tryin' to make ye jealous, Brian, please, it's not true, none of it's true!'

His car accelerated away, leaving her crucified on the cross of her revelations. After a moment she ran up to her apartment, wig in hand and flung herself on the bed and cried out across the streets of Dublin.

That night she couldn't rest. Her thoughts fell into the vagueness of near sleep, the blackness of her memories, the faces of her life, the mess her whole existence seemed to be in.

Rachel, her sister, pressing her nose against the glass. Her mother in bed with her father. She reflected on how in the early years she had made any excuse, any excuse to snuggle up and put her arms half way across her huge frame. Her mother always laughing at the latest one, hugging her till she'd nearly smother her. The arguments from downstairs in the kitchen when her father came home, the kindness in her father's eyes, the long walks with him telling her about all the animals that came to the surgery. And then Wallace and how he changed everything in her mother.

She opened her eyes. She knew she could not shut her brain down and every time she tried she was caught further down the pit of her memories, caught in a circle like a molecular structure bound by the rules of physics, knowing that she would never escape into sleep, a deep sleep that she craved.

She wanted Brian to touch her, brush his lips against her cheek, put his fingers through her hair, play with the strands, to tie little knots with his fingers, the way he always did. Pull her face towards him. Push his eyes into her face, leave the pain and fill the void with love and the smell of his cigars. To hold him, yes, oh yes, to hold him tight.

Faces re-appeared. Please Jesus, help me sleep just for a moment. Why did they leave each other? Why did Mummy go? Why did Daddy cut himself away? Why did she have to tell him about Valerie? Why to make him jealous! To make him love her more!

She imagined her father laughing, looking through a window, pointing at her saying:

'I told you Jenny, I warned you.'

She saw Brian on top of her and the hurt in his eyes. Turning to one side she grasped the pillow tight, knowing, feeling, that she was forever doomed to this sleepless shallow land where the past controlled. She relived the desperate moaning crying that came out of her when the doctor told her she would have to undergo chemotherapy.

When she had finished smoking, she sat up and cried and thought back to the lump against her kidney that had become inoperable and inflammatory, how they told her that it had become rapid growth cancer, how chemotherapy would be the only option and radiotherapy afterwards.

She though about how it had all started with the needle biopsy and the time spent waiting for the diagnosis. She thought of decay and death in Belfast.

She relived the dark of her unhappy upbringing.

* * *

August.

She removed her wig, ran her fingers over tufts of hair, stared into the mirror at her eyes, nose, and her mouth and couldn't understand why she was looking at herself, in such detail. In a moment she saw what other people saw. She watched her own reflection like a photograph and no matter how many times she tried again to catch that picture she never succeeded.

'If ye die, I'll kill ya!' she cried to her reflection, trying to make herself laugh.

Maybe that bastard Brian could show her, be the mirror, tell her what she was about, look into the face that was in the mirror, tell the face what she was searching for, define, lay down, explain to her what her life was and could be.

Maybe as she looked into the mirror she could even peel away her skin and find out what was behind those eyes that stared back at her. But she'd said to him so many times:

'When ye leave me, I get so lonely.'

'When ye leave me, I get so lonely.'

'When ye leave me I get so lonely.'

She'd warned him. She moved slowly to the kitchen sink

and poured boiling water into her coffee and stared into the black cup and let her anger settle.

Was he thinkin' about her … ?
Did he miss her?
Did he need her as much as she needed him?
Did he care enough to understand her predicament?
Where was he?
Who was he with?
Did he love her?
When he was inside his wife, was he thinkin' of her?
The anger.
Her anger.

One week without that man, one week of pain. He'd said that to her, four weeks of pain for every week of happiness. He'd said it to her in July in some restaurant, in a casual moment the way you'd throw a stone into a pond to see if the ripples would end up coming back at you. She knew exactly what he meant.

When it's over, it's over and it's only over when the screwdriver stops turning inside you, that it's over. But for her the screwdriver turned and the knot in her tightened.

* * *

She went to Waterstones in Dawson Street. She was inside the bookshop under the staircase, lost in a novel, deep where the words carried her on a journey away from herself. She was low but she felt the beat around her. She'd told him enough times about this place, he must have known that at some stage she'd be there.

From the front door he saw her and walked to her.

'Where have you been?' he asked.

She turned around, looked straight through him. 'Leave me alone.'

'Hold on a minute, hold on Jenny, hold on a sec.'

She put the book down.

'I said leave me alone.'

'Hold on a sec, I've done nothing, what are you going on about?'

He felt her elbow.

'Don't ye dare touch me, I said leave me alone.'

She turned around and made for Grafton Street, he went after her shouting.

'Come on, Jenny, what's going on? You haven't been in your flat for days, where the hell have you been? I want to talk about this.'

They walked through Hibernian Way moving in and out of the crowd, he tried to keep up with her.

'Look, this is silly, can't we talk? At least you owe me that.'

She stopped and swivelled around to face him.

'Don't ye ever say that I owe ye ... I owe ye nothin' ... Fuckin' nothin'.' she screamed out.

Heads turned. She made quick time. He let her go and she ran on a bit and turned, her hands on her hips.

'Please Brian, get out of my life. Don't be such a wee pest.'

It was as though it had been rehearsed, laid out to hurt him, delivered with the avenging bitterness of someone deeply aggrieved.

'Are you serious?' he asked biting his lip.

'Yeah, don't come near me, just leave me alone!'

It worked.

* * *

Days later, Frank and Brian sat in Devitt's Cusack Stand on Lower Camden Street right across from her flat. They could see her window.

'I'm not saying anything, I'm only saying that you seem to be losing control,' Frank said.

'What do you mean? You should spend less time thinking about me and more time trying to sort out the rats in the bakery.'

'I'll deal with the rats,' Frank said.

'Well you'd want to before the Eastern Health Board deal with us.'

Brian took his Guinness, licked the cream from his lips and said, 'It's going to rain, I'm sure it's going to rain.'

Brian wanted the water more than ever, if the rain came she would return to him.

'Fuckin' rain, it's always fuckin' raining. This is the worst summer, the worst! I'm glad it's nearly over,' Frank said.

'It's too late anyway to go back, I know I've made a mistake but I'm not going to lose her now.'

Frank turned to him.

'Brian I'm not paid to look at faces, but, well, yours says it all, I'm telling you, you'd want to be careful.'

As Frank said this, he looked up at the window across the street.

'You'll lose everything, my father used always say, 'Frank you watch your back in life and you'll live long and happy.'

He paused.

'Money has legs, and that girl's in the Olympics and I'll tell you one thing, she'll get gold, silver and bronze. I've told you before, she's high maintenance, the business can't afford her.'

They finished their pints.

'All I'm saying is you're having a cheque-book relationship, it's not right, it's not real.'

'She's got a hold on me and that's the God's honest truth, Frank, I can't seem to resist her, she's a drug I never knew existed.'

'A drug!' he laughed. 'She's fuckin' poison, take enough and you're dead. Remember the parachute ... I'm just saying it straight, you know the saying, true love may die but herpes lives forever.'

He continued:

'Brian listen, you're too involved, you should start to control them, like me. Lao Tsu says ... A good slave only needs to see the shadow of the whip. Listen, that girl is evolving through you and you're letting her do that. She's a rough stone. She'll ruin you. I've told you before Ciara is the real diamond. You're crazy.'

Brian slapped him on his back.

'Thanks, I don't need the advice.'

The light went on in her flat.

'She's home, look!'

Brian stood up, the smell of her in his nostrils. Frank raised his eyes and shook his head, but in a way anticipating the action.

'Oh here we go, look sit down will you and bide your time, that woman's in no hurry, and neither are you.'

* * *

Brian was out the door with fierce love in his eyes, hell bent on the girl and his heart thumping like a locomotive. Frank still at the bar counter, waiting for more insanity.

He ran across the road and approached the door outside her apartment, pressing the bell gently at first and looking up at the lighted window. He pushed it again, not letting the pressure off. The window above his head opened and a million knives, forks and spoons came out. He stood there with all the metal flying about him, crashing about the ground, bouncing off his head, his shoulders. He backed away from the bell and shouted, 'Jesus, what are you doing? Jenny c'mon, open the door.'

Her voice came out from the window:

'Go away, fuck off and leave me alone will ye?'

This was her game, her anger.

He began to pick up the cutlery piece by piece. Frank stood outside the pub laughing. Suddenly his face transformed. He roared at Brian to get out of the way.

Brian's face turned slowly to look up. Jenny screamed.

'Ye can stuff yer wee present!'

He saw the goldfish bowl coming through the air, like a football, and side-stepped. It hit the ground. The crash, and splintered glass flying, the goldfish wriggling on the pavement, sucking for life. Brian disbelieving and the shock of it written all over his face. Jenny lean out of the window screaming,'My fish, my fish. Oh my God, look what ye've made me do.'

Frank outside the pub, buckled up with laughter. Brian running towards him.

'She's crazy for sure, water, water, Frank, I won't let them die.'

And the two of them were back in the pub. The barman who had witnessed it exclaimed, 'I've seen it all now'.

Water, water, pints, anything, quick.' Brian shouted to him.

He got his water in pint glasses and dashed across the road, the water spilling all over the place and the cars braking. He picked up the goldfish, some of them wriggling in his fist, others slithering out. The partners on their hands and knees, swearing as they tried to feed the fish into the four glasses of water.

'Squeeze them, Frank, squeeze them, Jesus they're slippy, there's one over there, I can't believe she did that.'

The fish were flip-flapping over the cutlery. A car parking attendant came over pointing at one of the fish and said in a monotone, 'I think one of them is going to go down that drain.' he pointed.

Sure enough it was on the verge. They walked back to the pub with the glasses full of fish and Brian set them up on the counter in a line.

'Are you sure we got them all? There should be ten of them, hold on.'

'Yeah they're all there,' Frank counted.'Ten.'

On the counter there were eight pint glasses of water. The fish swam inside them, all the customers watched and the barman scratched his chin; they didn't teach him this in the early days. Frank took a sup of Guinness.

'I can't believe she did that, I know I was giving you a hard time about her but I can't believe she did that.'

After a moment Brian, breathless, said, 'Don't worry about her for the moment. Listen, ring the fiddle player we met the other day?'

'The one on Henry Street?'

Brian pulled out a piece of paper and gave it to his partner.

'That's his number, tell him to come straight away, tell him to get the other lads he was with last Saturday, tell him it's the donut man. He'll know.'

Frank stood up and headed for the phone. Brian shouted after him:

'And tell him to bring the box player and the pipes.'

'What do you mean?'

'I mean a session, a fuckin' session, what do you think I mean?'

'Where?' Frank asked.

Brian looked across the road at the open window.

After some moments Frank returned.

'They're coming alright, I tell you something, by the sounds of it we'll have half of Henry Street here, they're all in that fiddle player's flat rehearsing for a wedding or something, he said they're coming straight down.'

Frank stopped and took some of his drink, staring at the fish.

'You're a mad bastard, do you know that Brian O'Neill, what are we goin' to do with these?'

'Never mind these, you wouldn't go over there Frank and soften her up? I mean Jesus, she'll go fuckin' mad if she sees me again. Tell her we've saved all the fish that should do it ... Will you go over, will you talk some sense into her?'

There was a roar from a circle of men at a table.

'Will you be getting the chips with them?' looking at the fish.

The two boys laughed.

'You know how I feel about her, Brian, this time only.'

He directed his finger at Brian's conscience. In the background Elton John sang:

'I hope you don't mind, I hope you don't mind,
this is your song, you're the sweetest thing, you
can tell everybody, that you're the only one.'

Brian's face stared through the pint glasses in front of him and it was clear he was besotted with pictures of love and lust and Jenny.

After fifteen minutes Frank returned.

'We're away, we're away, the boys are over there, I met them outside.'

Brian looked at him.

'Jesus did you talk to her? What did she say? I mean did she ask if I was alright? Did she say anything? Did she kick you out? How come you were so long?'

Frank turned around and said,'She's into you, do I have to spell it out. You're a goner, she's got you, the hook's in your belly not your heart'.

The two of them finished their pints. Brian looked at the barman.

'Keep an eye on those for us will you,' he said, pointing at the fish.

'Ah come on.'

Brian was serious.

'Twenty-four hours, if these fish are not out of here by tomorrow night, I'm throwing them out,' the barman said.

'I tell you what ...' said Brian, 'Give us three large bottles of Paddy.'

He opened a bottle and poured whisky into the glasses of fish.

'They'll sleep!' he laughed at the barman

Outside the flat there was a crowd of people.

'Are you lot with the musicians?'

'No, we're playing,' said one of them and added, 'But they're with us.'

The man nodded his head at a crowd of people coming

towards them. The door of the building was half-open. People entered the apartment. They came from everywhere, from flats, from the street, from the pubs, arriving with their pints and their hope, and inside was the biggest session with banjos, guitars, fiddles and violins. The accordion wheezing, violins screeching out, the spoons clicking, three bodhrans and the uileann pipes. The screech of celebration all about the place.

That night they played jigs, reels and more jigs and the *Walls of Limerick* and *The Siege of Ennis* and the dancing was wild and the *craic* was wild with women on the table lifting their dresses and the sweat pouring from them, the men throwing themselves about the place with the tap dancing and the ferocious happiness that came from the deep history of the music.

Brian and Jenny in the adjoining bedroom and her legs up around him. He carrying her weight in his hands and digging his fingers into the flesh of her ass and pumping into her soft wetness and her against the bedroom wall. She felt the bodhran in her ears and she swore she was going to come. She whispered sweet joy into his ear and her fingers wrapped into the back of his head and the music was going away and she couldn't hear it anymore. All she could hear was the beat of the bodhran and the sounds inside her own head and the pulse of blood racing around her brain.

She was with him, taking him, letting him into the reaches of her longing where even she had never been, every thrust taking her further and further into the dream place and she reached another land, another time where she floated, floated away and she didn't want it, and she did, and she didn't, and she did. She breathed fast and hard into him and the moaning and then the soft scream.

Outside the frenzy of the music carrying everyone up. The sweat streaming down faces as the music raced quicker and quicker.

The flat was destroyed, the day was destroyed, everything was forgotten, the joy, the wild, wild Celtic eyes. The orgasm that they were all having. Brian and Jenny banging against the wall, burning away all their rows, all their differences, all the fever of their loss and all the pain and all the hurt and all the memories of hours spent dreaming, thinking, wondering and the sheer honesty of their lovemaking laying all the questions to rest, burning them all away.

* * *

It was two o'clock that morning, quiet with little wind and there was a pleasant warmth in the air. He had the window open and the smoke from his cigar drifted out. Streetlights blazed clear through.

When he got into the driveway he looked at his house. All the lights were out. He opened the door, he put the keys on the hall table and entered the kitchen. Sensing something, he doubled back and rushed upstairs. The door to the bathroom was closed but a light came out from underneath.

'Ciara? Ciara are you in there?'

He turned the door handle and the door clicked open. She lay in the water motionless. He was surprised and looked at his wife, her eyes turned down, mascara running down her cheeks. The suds had melted.

'How long have you been here?'

She didn't answer, she found the soap and started to finger it, rolling it over in her hand.

It's half past two in the morning, what's going on?' he asked.

She said nothing. He went over to the toilet seat, brought the lid down, sat on it and leaned over.

'What's happened? Why are you crying?'

'I'm not crying.'

'What's wrong?'

She didn't look at him.

'I told you, there's nothing wrong.'

She put both her arms on the side of the bath and looked

resolutely at the water, her eyes on a soap sud clinging to the side. He stood up and went over to the edge.

'Ciara!'

She didn't respond. He put his fingers into the water.

'Jesus, the water's cold, it's freezing.'

He put his hands underneath his wife's armpits and lifted her out of the bath, got a large towel and draped it over her. She stood out of the bath, shivering.

'God almighty I don't believe you, you're bloody frozen, what's got into you? How long have you been in there for?'

He started to rub her down, her teeth chattering and him bringing his hands all about her white shrivelled skin. She didn't look at him as he brought the cloth over her legs, her bottom, her back, the wet strands of hair that were plastered to her shoulders, her breasts, her tummy. He went over everything again. His wife, his beautiful wife.

'Okay, c'mon into bed, I'm making you hot milk.'

He brought her into their bedroom, perplexed and unsure. He saw his Visa-card bill on the side of the bed, an amount highlighted with marker. She climbed into bed, after some time he returned with a hot drink.

'Why are you so quiet?' He asked staring at the bill. She waited for some moments and turned to him.

'Who did you take out for a meal?'

'I dunno, when was it?'

'The fourteenth of last month, in a Chinese restaurant, who was she Brian?'

'What are you're saying?'

But she turned away as though she didn't want to know anymore. She finished her milk.

'I was just thinking,' she said.

'Thinking what?'

'About us.'

'What about us?'

He took off his clothes, folding them onto a chair at the end of their bed.

'You're distant, not the same, we're not close.'

'What do you mean? I don't know what you're saying.'

'That's just it, before you would have known what I was saying, now it's as if you don't want to know what I'm saying.'

He slipped between the sheets away from his wife. She continued talking.

'I never seem to know what you're thinking anymore, you always seem to be holding something back, Brian, you've gone cold on me!'

She was deep into his eyes.

'I don't know you anymore.'

There was total silence and as though to put the nightmare out of his head he switched the light off.

'Are you sure you don't want to tell me?' she asked in a quiet voice.

'He said after a silence, 'You're my wife, I love you'.

'I rang the bakery this afternoon. You weren't there, I was talking to one of the cleaners, she told me you'd left but you haven't been home ... do you know what I'm trying to say.'

'Yeah.'

'Eileen hurt herself.'

'What?'

The light went back on.

'Is she all right?'

'She's in bed asleep, we've spent all afternoon in the hospital waiting for an x-ray and I couldn't contact you, Brian, you were nowhere to be found. It's as if you don't know about us, as if ... I've suddenly discovered you're all wrong for me.'

She started to cry.

'It's been so terrible today, it's been so bad. You should have been with us, you should have been here, don't you understand? ... they're your children, I'm your wife.'

Brian left the bed and walked to his daughter's room and sat by the bed stroking his little girl's forehead.

Maybe it was at this time he realised that he'd been

spending too much time with that girl, facing his own deceit, realising at last that maybe deceit is about stealing time, telling lies and bringing pain to himself and others close to him.

* * *

The following evening, he brought her to the Gate Theatre to see Chekov's *Uncle Vanya*.

She'd been unusually quiet all day and in the car on the journey into town she looked out at Dublin, her face full of silent remorse, inquisition and suffering. Half way through the first half of the play he turned to see tears washing down; the glance through her watered eyes that confessed her anguish. He grabbed her, pulled her out of her seat and walked her to the refreshment bar where they tried to bury the corpse of his infidelity. She had her arms wrapped around him and through her tears she uttered the truth.

'You're my man, you're my man, you're my man.'

* * *

> *'Brian I can't go on living like this, What's happening, what's wrong with us ... you can't live your silence through me and the children, either you go away and get yourself sorted out or I go, one or the other, I can't go on living like this.'*

*

> *One afternoon his woman is standing in the garden putting the clothes on the line.*
> *He's helping her with a huge duvet cover.*
> *They finish clipping the cover to the line.*
> *She picks up a basket of clean clothes and says, 'I'm so unhappy.'*

'You've no reason.'
'I have every reason, this is about you, me, the children, it's our lives you're destroying, don't destroy our marriage Brian, I need a husband, and I need a companion. I need you.'

*

Later in the carwash, he chews on his lip.
She turns to him and says: 'It's okay for you, you get into this car, drive into another world where I don't exist, the children don't exist, and everything is different for you and then, and then you are so easily distracted, it's as if we don't exist, and I'm the one Brian who has to put up with it, it's like I'm dealing with another child.'

*

She's having her period, she feels at her worst, swamped by the cycle of her hormones, her mind falls prey to a chasm of uncertainty about them and the truth is she cannot comes to terms with the unpredictability of his behaviour and this, this is the worst part, her expectations had been destroyed. Yet there is the dilemma of seeing him being good with the children, caring, responsible.
If she could only bring this man to his senses because for sure, her love is good love, her way is a good way, her affection is solid and her vows sacrosanct.

*

One afternoon she doesn't know quite why she said it, why she let it out of her. But he'd been silent at dinner and snappy when she'd been trying to be kind to him. She says, 'There are so many things that have gone wrong, I don't know you anymore Brian, this has become like one of those 'vision no sound' marriages we see when we go to restaurants.'

*

'Brian am I getting too old for you?'
'Don't be ridiculous.'
'Well, what is it?'
'It's nothing. I don't know what you're going on about ... age doesn't matter.'
'God, you should listen to yourself. You sound as though it doesn't matter to you. Brian, everyone's afraid of growing old.

*

One evening, she decides to put it to him, mustering up courage and strength she says, 'I've done everything except tell you what I think of your answers'.
She gets her lipstick, goes to the window of the kitchen and writes on it in big letters - LIAR - and replaces the lipstick in her bag.
She looks into his eyes and says, 'You don't know how much courage it took to do that.'
'Jesus, Ciara did you have to do that?'
'I think it would be better for everyone if you go and sort yourself out, I can't take it any more, please, you've got to do this yourself. Look, it's either you or us.'
He tells her he'll go to the country, and she replies 'I don't care where you go but do something.'
He stares at the writing on the window.
I can't understand you,' she says. 'Sometimes when

we're dancing you're miles away ... I can't dance with you anymore when you're not with me, don't you understand that the dancing is over, Brian?'

* * *

He brought Ciara for lunch to Pasta Fresca on Chatham Street. They were given a table beside the window and they looked out at women carrying designer-label bags. A tall waitress put some bread in front of them.

'Do you think I don't know you?' she asked, leaning into him and continued. 'Do we understand each other anymore?'

The waitress approached and poured a glass of wine. He motioned for her to fill the two glasses. She continued.

'You must remember, when we got married, we were young, we didn't know what we know now, we've grown into it, into us, I can't sit back when I know in my heart that there is something wrong.'

He played with the cutlery and said. 'You say we don't understand each other, well you must realise that I'm worried like hell about the business.'

'You don't have to talk, I know what's going through your head,' she replied.

He sipped his wine.

'Go on.'

'You're up, the world is full of lights and the party begins, you're down, it's a funeral, but you can't let money come between us, if it is money?'

'What are you implying?'

'Brian I share your emotions, and you've got to understand I'm helpless if you fold. Can't you see what's happening to you? You come into the house, it's like a railway station, as soon as you've eaten you're gone.'

She took some wine, they ordered some food. The waitress left.

'Well, are you going to tell me?'

'I've told you the truth.'

'Brian, I just want to say one thing, if you're having a relationship ... someone's going to get hurt.'

'That's crap, you've nothing to worry about.'

She raised her voice, 'I'm your wife, damn you, I've a right to you, I've a right to your love. I've a right to know you care about me!'

'Jesus, Ciara, that's enough!'

He threw his napkin on the table and rose, she implored him to sit. After they had taken some food she said: 'Sometimes you can be so cruel'.

'I don't want to get tied down like that, it'll destroy us.'

He took some more wine and broke some bread.

'I'm not going to be one of those husbands who has to answer for every move he makes, that's the way it is, darling.'

She lifted her eyebrows.

'You know I've never tried to impose anything like that on you, you've always had your head in this relationship, and do you know who's telling you that, yes that's right, Mrs O'Neill the woman who took your name, the woman who gave you your children, you're lucky I love you the way I do, nobody would put up with it, nobody else.'

She put her fingers up in front of him.

'I don't even get a ring!'

Brian fiddled with some bread.

'I'm sorry Ciara' he said

'I don't want you or me to get hurt that's all.'

'Jesus, Ciara.'

'Brian I love you, don't you see, and ... and ... and you've got to treat me like a wife, like your woman.'

She smiled awkwardly.

'Listen Mrs O'Neill, I love you.'

He leaned over the table and kissed her.

She buried her head in her hands. Through her hair he could see the tears flowing down. She looked into his face and said, 'I don't know what's happening to us Brian, it's not the same anymore, I just don't have the same feelings. You've wrecked all my feelings for you.'

She began to cry heavily but the tears were silent. She dabbed her cheek with the cloth napkin but the water wouldn't stop. He left money on the table, took her by the arm and walked her out of the restaurant, bringing her emotion and sorrow onto the streets of Dublin where a thousand people swallowed them up.

* * *

Jenny ran to him.

'Ye can't do this, I'm on my knees, ye can't let me down, I love ye, I love ye, I'll kiss yer feet, the ground ye walk on, just don't go, not now, I've given ye my all Brian, please don't go, I never wanted to come between you and Ciara, never!'

He cut in.

'It's all coming out of me, coming out of my pores, coming out of my skin, Jesus, I can't go by one minute without thinking about you, listen to me!'

He lowered his voice. He went over to her, bent over and put her face in his hands.

'Jenny all I know is that I'm hurting her and I won't do that. I'm not going to let our marriage become another statistic!'

She looked at him unsure about where she was, as though his words had abandoned the truth and his eyes were lying to her and she knew that in her own reality, that in her own crazy logic that what he was saying was not true and that it was not happening to her.

'No, no, I'm not lettin' ye go, ye can't dump me, I'm not a piece of meat, I need ye.'

She put her arms tight around his neck.

'Don't leave me, please! Don't leave me, not now!'

This is reality darling, I'm hurting Ciara too much, don't you understand I'm not going to do it anymore and that's final, please don't make this difficult.'

She moved to the bed and sat on it, with her long legs and suit that she'd put on to make a change for him. She looked up and asked,

'What will ye do?'

'I dunno, same as usual I suppose, this and that.'

'Where will ye go?'

'What do you mean, I'm going nowhere, I've got to run my business, the world is turning.'

'Yer such a brute!' she said.

But she cried away from him:

'Ye really are cuttin' me off.'

'Jenny I've got to stop it.'

'Yer weak, yer blind, ye can't see the difference between me and yer guilt.'

'It's not about guilt.'

'It is.'

'Yer weak, ye can't handle havin' two women, yer a weak man.'

She banged his chest with her fists as she repeated the words.

'Weak, weak, weak. Ye can't handle two women and yer guilt is killin' ye.'

'I've never felt guilt.'

'Yer lyin'.'

She moved away from him.

'Ye just want to make a decision and walk away from it.'

'Yeah maybe.'

'Ye came in here with that decision didn't ye, didn't ye?'

'Jenny stop.'

'No I won't, ye bastard, look at me, I love ye.'

'Jesus, take it easy.'

'But I love ye. '

She was up close.

'Jenny don't do this to me.'

'I'm not doin' anythin' to ye, yer only thinkin' about

yerself, yer always thinkin' about yerself.'

'Don't make me walk out of here feeling bad.'

He went over to the wig-stand and fingered the hair.

'Yer wife's suffocatin' ye.'

He expressed surprise.

'Fuck you,' he said and walked.

She shouted after him, 'Brian, no Brian, I'm sorry, I didn't mean it, please Brian!'

She sobbed quietly at the top of the stairs, knowing that something true had been taken from deep inside her.

She looked out of her window and felt the soft warmth of an autumnal sun.

Kissing the Orange

Autumn

Autumn's hand moved across the country devouring it in its mantle of rust and Jenny took the Dart out to Howth, walked to the Baily Lighthouse and sat on a rock overlooking the bay. She watched the ferry ease its way through the piers at Dun Laoghaire and she listened to the echo of the jets passing behind her, over Howth harbour. She ran her finger across her arm feeling the down and thought about the circle of this obsession from which she couldn't escape. She thought about the future. She looked at the still sea lapping against the rocks.

Tomorrow a new day. Tomorrow without kisses, without even the fuel of laughter to counter the loneliness of her isolation. Tomorrow an emptiness to be filled with the ravings of her imagination.

She watched the seagulls breaking the breeze, their wing tips flickering, their necks stretched out, calling.

Again she felt afraid, afraid of life, afraid of death, afraid of returning to the Belfast City Hospital, of Wallace, of her mother, of Brian's impulsiveness, of herself and the fear wasting her equilibrium, bringing her to the depths of this new almost suicidal depression.

It humiliated her that she couldn't face it all, face her own weaknesses, that once she could rely on courage but it had dissipated out of her so that again she had ended up making a terrible mistake with a married man.

She hated him now as much as she had loved him then.

Was it always going to be this way.

Maybe if it hadn't rained so much during their time.

Maybe if she hadn't stayed so long with him.

Maybe if she hadn't lost her temper.

Maybe if she hadn't existed at all.

She watched the traffic wind across the lip of Clontarf, the tide sucking in the Liffey and the Dublin Mountains with their masts and their quarries and the Pigeon House chimneys goalposting into the evening sky, the Obelisk, a pin on top of Killiney Hill.

She reflected to the early years, her father, going through

all the sick animals and the way he'd show her how to work with them, the fishing trips and when he caught one how he'd remove the hook and throw it back in and how she wished that he could get the hook out of her and help her restart, wounded but free.

It occurred to her that it was the diagnosis that had made her so manic, forced her to live every moment, the reality that it could return to thwart her hope, her future, take away her best years, even reflecting on it, on the course of injections, made her touch her breasts feeling for lumps, recalling the curse of that genetic inheritance.

It made her feel the apprehension of going again under the anaesthetic, the masks, the eyes, the count and the knife.

In a way she wished she could cry but she knew she would need the stimulus of music to force the tears. She wished she could get angry but the seagulls called and their grace enthralled her. She wished she could return to the ritual of their love, show him that the loyalty of her passion was limitless. But the air was cold.

She thought about something Brian had said: 'Maybe the best way to be together, is to be apart.'

God, that man had brought her trouble, but also awoken something strange inside her and she realised as she watched the birds that she was still with him, still talking to him as though in his absence it had actually become a much stronger bond.

He had been right.

She watched the ferry disappear behind the terminus and as she rocked back and forth, her head resting in her arms, she stared up to the dark clouds rolling in over Dublin and the seagulls swirling across the contours of her own tortured imaginings.

* * *

That same evening Ciara parked the car at the Blue Light up

high in the Dublin Mountains. She got out, leaned against the bonnet and looked over Dublin Bay, to the Obelisk on Killiney Hill, to the harbour walls that pencilled out into the sea, to the long slug of Howth and the Baily Lighthouse, to the ferry that sailed into Dun Laoghaire.

She thought about how she'd carry on without him, about survival, about providing for the children, about returning to medicine.

She questioned everything.

Had she changed so much?

Had he changed beyond her?

Was the bed she'd made into their marriage, soiled, tarnished and ridden with infidelity or was it the course of her imagination?

What had she done to deserve this?

Would they end up divorced ... another sad divorce?

Had she been too involved with the children?

Had she forgotten his needs?

Were his desires becoming unrecognisable to her?

Had she become so utterly self-absorbed that she'd missed it?

Missed the moment.

What was that moment?

Did it exist at all or was it about a million moments?

When would he attack her with his desire, make love with her and make her feel the lust which belonged with her love ... make the two inseparable again?

She looked at the clouds coming in over Howth to cover the light of their love, their care, their union. She looked at the ferry edging into Dun Laoghaire and she wondered whether that evening he would impress the kisses on her that he'd done before all the rain had started. She wondered whether even that night the rain might hold off and he would lick her tongue, her gums, her teeth, the roof of her mouth.

She looked at the church in Dun Laoghaire, the cranes that had started to appear all over Dublin, the glazed sea like a pool of rock water, the film of smog over Tallaght and wondered if he was in the bakery at all.

She questioned his sincerity, no, maybe she was being paranoid. She went back to their wedding, to the speeches, to her father and mother and the photographs in St. Stephen's green, to the children and she thought how he had been with her and she really felt then that all that time with him must add up to something.

She watched the ferry slip in against its moorings and the clouds come in over Dublin and she felt the sprinkles against her skin and looked up to feel the water dancing into her eyes and she thought how easy it would be to take the children and leave him and the rain and go somewhere warm where she could set up and start over.

Later she visited the church in Swords and prayed for hours, prayed that Jesus would help him become an adult, a lover, a father, that reason would prevail, that his crazy impulsiveness would disintegrate in the mumblings of her invocation.

* * *

That night he sat beside the plinth of the Obelisk on Killiney Hill. He looked at his shoes and turned his gaze out to the limpid sea. He felt their arms around him and the warm air from their lungs touch and brush against his skin. He felt their hair, eyes, smiles and thought how sometimes in the dark he woke up unsure who was lying beside him, breathing into his ear, whispering with the same voice, the voice that gave him warmth, succour and strength, the voice to which he now listened, calling him from Howth Hill and the Dublin Mountains, a clamour rippling across the sea and the suburbs, carrying the distorted messages of confusion, devotion, anguish and solitude.

He knew that the decision had been made and that he would live with it and he knew that the smell would be different, that the touch would never be the same. He looked at the ferry edging its way into Dun Laoghaire Harbour and felt the shudder of reality in the droplets of rain that touched his forehead. He reasoned that his destiny lay in self-control, that his pilgrimage was over, that he had to act, that he had to accept the consequences of his own actions, that the rain would eventually subside and the sunshine of reason and responsibility return.

He looked up and saw swallows in jagged flight and he thought that maybe if the sun did come out they would fly in a line, straight as an arrow.

* * *

September.

Her mother's rounded face was lined with anger, in her eyes the blank stare of one who distrusted all. Wide brown-grey eyes of terror behind cavernous eyebrows, heavy lips and short-stubbed lashes. The mouth small with thin lips, her nose reaching high up onto the forehead, puffed cheeks covered strong bones. Two lines furrowed craggily past the corners of her lips and on top of this unhappy face, thick red hair neatly clipped and all set over broad shoulders.

This matriarch was obeyed by all. When Jenny was growing up, her mother used to fold her thick arms and scream, 'Catch yerself on, catch yerself on girl.'

She will not, and has not been disobeyed by any of her children, hers was the word, she protected because she owned, she owned because she gave birth.

Jenny sat down.

'Who is he?' her mother asked with her strong Northern accent.

Jenny looked across her flat at her mother silhouetted in front of the window.

'I've told ye, a friend, he's a friend.'

But her eyes were down, her mother reeled around, her

eyes wild, the stained teeth opened.

'Where does he live, girl? Where does he live? Listen to me when I talk to ye.'

'I told ye, I don't know.'

'Look we have his phone number, where does he live?'

'I told ye he's a friend. That's all.'

That wasn't enough, Jenny stood up from the chair beside her wig-stand and moved backwards towards the fireplace, watching her mother closely. She turned her face and nervously fingered an ink bottle on the table.

In a moment, her mother rushed towards her and took a hold of her jumper, rolled it around her fist and pulled her back onto the chair. Jenny looked up, she knew what was coming.

'Don't hit me, please don't hit me!' she begged.

In a sweep of her arm the woman brought the palm of her hand against the side of her daughter's head.

'Listen young woman, ye tell me what I want to know or I'll get someone to deal with ye,' she screamed.

Jenny was frightened and hurting deep inside, where the memory of all this would linger, her head aching from the knuckle blow, her ears singing. She looked up into her mother's eyes.

'Why are ye hittin' me like this?' she asked.

'I'll tell ye, I'll tell ye, ye little lady, ye need to come to yer senses and furthermore I'll hit ye when I want, right. Now ye tell me, do ye hear, where does he live?'

She brought her fist across her daughter's cheek, catching the skin with the stone of her ring. She screamed, 'Wise up, girl wise up. Tell me, whooo is he? Where does he live? C'mon, wise up girl.'

Driblets of blood leaked from Jenny's nose and began to trickle over her mouth. Her mother pulled her up from the seat, twisting her towards her.

'It's hurtin', yer hurtin', yer hurtin' me!' Jenny shouted.

'I'll deal with ye now if ye don' tell me.'

Jenny fell back and instinctively her mother reached over and tugged, with spit coming from her mouth and teeth clenched she dragged her across the room to the fireplace.

'No, No, No!' Jenny pleaded, but she slipped and smacked her cheek against the edge of a chair.

Her mother bent close to her. 'I'm doing it for yer own good, ye know, yer own good!'

Jenny was in pain, disorientated and listless. She tried to hold onto the mantelpiece, her legs swaying, her stomach convulsing. Her mother grabbed her, hauling her across the room and pushed her into the bedroom where she fell beside the bed repeating:

'I hate ye, I hate ye, I hate ye. All of yeu.'

'I'm doing it for yer own good, ye'll be comin' back to Dundonald, my wee girl.'

And for the next hour she went through the press drawers and the pockets of her daughter's clothes, searching for evidence, shouting: 'Yer my girl, remember that, my girl Jenny, my wee girl.'

Her posters, her fish, the ghost of her father, all silent witnesses to this violence.

* * *

She detested her flat now that it was full of violence, a scar on the tissue of her love.

She despised her mother, she loathed the summer. She hated everything that had been so pleasant before.

* * *

October.

Late afternoon. Brian took his car to Bray, to collect money from one of his customers, he ended up on the Esplanade with its blue poles and its long walk beside the Irish sea. The wind was up. He watched the sea coming in, covering the stones,

Kissing the Orange

sucking them into its belly as he walked towards Bray Head with it's crucifix staring down. The wind carried the drizzle of the sea-wash and it ran across his face into his eyes, nose, ears and left the taste of salt on his lips.

For over an hour he paced up and down, the beat of it pumping inside him, knowing that she had him, mind, body and soul.

He questioned if he had done the right thing by finishing it. He worried incessantly about her ability to fight it. He asked himself whether he should try to return into the coil of her love? Whether, in fact, she would allow him into her, to her care, to her soft smile that had transfixed him for so long, to the lips that had sucked his kiss, to the smiling eyes that had softened him, made him feel all right.

He doubted his strength. He missed her. He didn't know if he could control himself anymore.

He stayed there, looking out at the white horses rolling around on top of the sea, his hair flattened with water and it running down his back, into his shirt, into his conscience. He walked to the Carrig Bar with its dart-board, its high wooden stools, its walls covered in old lamps, guns and framed prints of the Wicklow Mountains.

The barman, a man with hands as big as a boxers, looked at him and smiled at the pools of water he left behind him:

'You're soaked.'

'I was walking.'

'You're asking for punishment out there.'

'A coffee thanks.'

'One coffee. It's whisky you need.'

'I don't feel like it, just a coffee.'

The barman made the drink. Brian had his head buried in his hands.

'You all right?' the barman asked.

No reply.

'I said are you all right?'

'All right, all right, of course I'm not fucking all right, Jesus

Christ man,' he exploded.

'Take it easy,' the barman said.

After a while Brian raised his head.

'Sorry.'

'Here look.'

The barman reached over and put a glass of whisky down in front of him.

'You get that into you son,' he said and watched Brian swallow.

'I always know when I get someone coming in the afternoon, he's got a problem ... afternoon drinkers!'

'You a psychic?'

'It's the rain ... our takings go up ... it's always the same ... we get trouble when it rains ... you watch yourself, son.'

Brian finished and stood up.

'You're a decent skin,' he called back at the barman and returned to his car.

He took the Peugeot out of the car park and headed back into Bray, but the railway barriers were down. He pulled up and switched on the stereo and listened to Deacon Blue.

The Dart train with its windows lit up started to move past and he saw her, was it her? Jesus Christ it was, for sure it was, with her tight blond hair, the unmistakable slant of her nose and her wide eyes. He sat upright as the barrier went up, put his foot to the floor and drove the car over the tracks into Bray.

He passed a car on his outside, the driver slammed his fist on his horn but Brian was possessed. In Bray he broke through three sets of traffic lights.

At the last one he charged through a red light at speed. A car emerged out from a side road, he swerved to avoid it, the engine burning up, the fierce demons of his madness pushing him and for ten minutes he went flat out on the Loughlinstown dual carriageway. Amidst a flurry of horns, he broke more lights until he reached the Killiney Dart station. He drove by the sea and into the station, braked, jumped out and ran to the ticket office.

'The train from Bray, has it arrived?'

'Which one is that?' the uniformed man said matter-of-fact and continued, 'There was a train here eight minutes ago, the next one …'

He didn't wait for the rest. He rushed into the car, started it up and made for Dublin, chasing this girl and her train. He drove down on the main road cutting through Sandycove, on through into Dun Laoghaire. He was sure he had caught flashes of the Dart on his right. He passed cars on both sides, like a man on a mission of life or death, he broke lights, he took horrendous chances and before he got into Blackrock the lights changed to red. He pulled the wheel of the car and took it up on the pavement back onto the main road heading into Booterstown.

Two container trucks blocked his way. Reversing the car, he charged it down on the wrong side of the road, his lights full on, his horn blaring and people jumped from death. As he got to Blackrock Park he swerved across the road, saw a gap, cut back in and made it over to the inside lane. Drivers disbelieved his lunacy. The Gardaí were on to him, the squad cars out with their blue lights and their sirens. But he had the advantage and seeing the train coming out of Booterstown station parallel to him, he passed out a stream of traffic that had lined up on his right to cross over the railway lines at Sandymount Gates.

As he reached the level crossing, the red and white barriers descended, A barrier hit the top of the car. He pulled up across the tracks, leaped out, gazing down the line at the green train coming towards him. People screamed, at him. He lifted his hand in the air. The train came to a halt. He broke into a sprint and ran down alongside on the chipped stones to the second last carriage. He reached up and banged on the glass window. She turned around. It was someone else.

* * *

Brian was arrested. He was pushed into the police station. A garda held him tight, both hands locked on his arm. A second garda clamped his fingers around the back of Brian's neck, forcing his head down. He was led past the hollow sound of grouped uniforms. Past six, seven of them staring at him, at charge sheets, at themselves.

A radio cut in. In a moment two of them moved out quickly and made for the station entrance, for a car and trouble. Brian was at a hatch.

'Empty your pockets.'

There was the pungent odour of disinfectant that neutralised the germs of another crime. In the background a radio gaggled. A garda marched him towards a solid door and he was thrown into a holding cell. In the corner of the room there was a toilet bowl set into concrete, inside it, urine and a plastic cup. The door closed behind him. On the walls graffiti on glossed light-brown paint, on the ceiling names burnt in with cigarettes, no Michelangelos here, only the egos of other minds.

He sat against a wall, an hour passed, maybe two, maybe a lifetime, time.

There was a hole in the door. Every now and again the light on the outside was blocked as an eye stared in. It withdrew. Footsteps and shouting. A large key was inserted into the lock, turning slow and easy. There were shouts. The door opened. They threw in a man, red hair matted to his head, skin covered in dried blood, a scar jagged over his eye as though someone had taken a Stanley knife, cut his face up like an apple and peeled the innocence of his boyhood away. The eyes wild, dancing with aggression and set deep into his forehead.

The heavy door shut and the key turned. The bloodied head of the man came straight at him swinging fists that caught him under the left side of his mouth, moving in and hitting Brian full on the bridge of his nose. He was making his mark, making his stake in the cell. This was his land, his country. Yeah, fear ruled and Brian stayed silent as eyes watched from the keyhole. He stood against the wall, maybe he was listening to the bells of the Angelus or maybe it was the ringing inside his head. He was stunned, sniffing, trying to keep the blood in. The man lunged at him going for the head butt.

'Stop, stop it, stop it, leave it out,' Brian shouted.

The man reeled around, stooped down, picked up the plastic cup out of the toilet bowl and threw the contents, spraying urine across the room. He side-stepped, shaking. As quick as it had started it subsided. The man got under a blanket and lay down. Brian leaned against a wall, staring into the middle distance, eyes locked on the wall.

'You come over here,' the man said.

'Fuck off!'

'You fuckin' come over here!' he screamed.

Brian stood up, knowing it would be a long fight.

The key went into the door. The door swung open and three gardai entered.

'C'mon you!'

The man stood up and walked out as though he'd done nothing. Fifteen minutes later Brian was called out and released on his own bail. He walked out of the station past Trinity College and up Dame Street to a Chinese restaurant. Oriental faces stared at his bloodied face. He took a seat.

'I'd like coffee, please!'

The waiter looked at him.

'No, no, we not serve coffee.'

He looked into the face.

'Please, I need a coffee.'

A head somewhere in the distance nodded, two Chinese men at a table nearby watched him, unsure. His swollen mouth could barely make the suck, and black coffee dribbled across his chin. A girl approached and gave him a paper napkin. As he drank, he touched his chin to make sure none of it fell on the table. His hair smelt of disinfectant.

It was a cool evening when only the feel and texture of a woman's gentleness could have brought him warmth.

But he was cold.

He was very cold. And the dream of Jenny's kisses was lost in the reality of his instinct for survival and the realisation of his stupidity.

* * *

It had rained for some time, the sweet drops of Autumn cool. By St. Stephen's Green there was a row of aluminium phone kiosks and there was Jenny's emptiness. She opened one of the doors and stepped into a pool of urine. For a moment the acrid odour filled her senses, drowning out the deep burning pain of her loss. And all this going through her head. Would he answer?

Would she say anything?

Would he talk to her at all?

She thought 'would he answer?'

She thought 'would he answer?'

She thought 'would he answer?'

The receiver shook against her ear, she remembered the coins, she'd forgotten the coins.

'Oh Jesus!'

'Hello Brian, Brian, hold on, wait ...'

She was cut off and it was his voice, it was Brian, yes, it was his sound.

She pulled coins out of her coat. Fumbling, dropping half of them. Some tissues fell, her heart dropped, she had the coins.

She tapped out the number, the coins fell.

'It's me .... Brian, I, I ... I'm sorry, it's not what ye think ... I know ... it's, oh please can't ye understand.'

She began to well up. There was silence and she listened.

'Please I need to see ye, I need ye, please, darling don't hang up please.'

She heard the click.

She shouted 'No, No, No, No, No!'

The receiver fell away from her hand, her knees began to bend, she dropped to the floor of the kiosk and sobbed uncontrollably, screaming out her anguish, and pain. The real Pain. Her face crippled with lines of loss and her tears fell down to mix with the urine.

* * *

LETTERS FROM JENNY

Brian
We've made a mistake and I know we've done the wrong thing, I know it, but you've got to understand it for both of us, you make me feel as though it was just me - you can't do that. I didn't mean to lead you up the wrong way, we've got to talk, can you ring or call to my place?

*

Brian
I gave you love when that's all I had. You don't know how badly I am. I hardly know how much to tell you I fucking hate you.
You bastard call me.

*

Brian
Do you know what you've done to me ... do you? I'm hurting ... don't you understand you've done this, you piece of shit.

He got up early every morning to open the post. There was one more letter. It arrived as he was getting ready to bring his daughter Eileen to school. He read it in the car. It read simply:

Brian, I hate you.

'Daddy what's that you're reading?' his daughter asked.
'Nothing,' he replied, 'Somebody died that's all.'

* * *

Jenny walked into McDaids to understand her past, to see him, to feel his eyes, to smell him, to re-live it.

She looked into faces and eyes of uncertainty watching her, eyes indifferent to her, eyes that reflected her turmoil.

She walked into the toilet, put her fingers under the cold tap and let the water run over them, her palms, her nails and her thin wrists. She went to the toilet, looked at a used tampon bloody and neglected colouring the water. She sat on the toilet seat and stared at the graffiti on the door and inscribed the words into her mind. She pissed and cleaned herself, flushed the toilet and went back to the sink, again she put her hands under the taps letting the cold drops waterfall over her fingers, her hands, her wrists, turning her fingers over and over in the soap, leaving the bubbles trail away from the tips and through the water she saw him dancing with his wife, his dancing. She imagined fierce controlled steps turning into an oblivion of movement. The man and his wife surrounded by the magic of the tango, the waltz, his arms octopusing around her own love smothering her own real passion for him, suffocating her, denying her, bringing her into the darkest vaults of hell, the darkest flame burning her over and over and over into the ashes of memory. A past suffocated by failure, a void filled by memories, the aura of hell, the dark of her own father's death, Brian's denial of her love, her mother's emotional disorder, her friend's weakness and the inspiration that maybe if she had children all this would go away and she could start out a new person, a new baby, a new Jenny. Produce a new generation, a love beyond her and

Kissing the Orange

beyond the sadness of Dublin and Belfast, become a heroine to herself, regenerate, repeat, destroy her mother's lonely hatred, destroy the hatred in herself, listen to the song of hope through the chords of her own offspring.

She lifted her head and stared into the cracked mirror where she had looked so often before and saw the face of someone she didn't want to see. She left the pub and walked to Bewley's, her hands still wet. He wasn't there. She sat and sipped coffee, watching people eat.

She walked up Grafton Street to a restaurant where they had eaten before but he wasn't there.

She went into HMV where he had brought her once to listen to the Waterboys on the headphones. She listened to music from the speakers, 'Tears for Fears', the band that reminded her of the tongue that licked the inside of her mouth, that discharged saliva into her throat that left her with the tang of love.

He wasn't there.

She stared into the faces of everyone and in her pain, she began to lose hope.

She walked to Waterstones and leafed through books without reading any of them. Waiting. Waiting for the feel of his presence. Waiting for the beat.

She returned to McDaids. To Bewley's. To 'The Bailey'. She heard conversations but no words. She remembered he'd told her about the Long Room in Trinity and she walked into the hall up to the glass cabinet, stared at the Book of Kells and the illustrations of St John, the eagle, she touched the harp. She walked to a bookcase and rested her head against the wood and cried.

Later that afternoon she went to a restaurant on Dawson Street, sure that he was sitting at one of the end tables, his back to her. She walked quickly, weaving in and around the tables, her eyes glowing, wide and expectant, approaching the table she touched him on the shoulder.

'Brian?'

He turned around. It wasn't him.

'I'm sorry, I'm sorry, I'm sorry,' she muttered.

She turned her head and walked out and across the street, oblivious to the traffic. Horns blared but she heard only the words of the song, 'Kiss me, my sweet.'

She thought the whole thing had been an illusion.

She went to a night-club on Leeson Street and felt nothing and everything, numb and expectant. She went to the toilet and lined her lips.

She mouthed with her reflection in the mirror, 'If ye die, I'll kill ya!'

She walked down a staircase and into the music, into a thousand faces of happiness.

She bought white wine and watched the night come alive with sound and dance. She stepped into a world of doubt, dreams, desire. She waited until she felt the death of her own longings in the reality of a myriad of eyes She watched dresses change with the sway of arms. She looked at threads of light reflecting against skin. She stared at girls, their lips open. She watched men spill drink. She sucked the grape and dreamed about another peace and the silence of her own longings. In a moment where the stimulus of the music crossed the beat inside her, she touched the past and became a corpse within her own energy. She cried beyond hope. She buried grief. She withdrew from the music, the words, the pulse, the dancers, the efforts of men to talk to her.

She waited until it all stopped inside her.

She walked out into the music of the rain and the chorus of droplets against the pavement. She passed by the basements of other clubs and listened to fevered guitars.

She walked by the Royal canal and watched the surface of the water come alive. It occurred to her that drowning would be a simple way to die, that the water would fill her lungs, her bowels, her eyes, her stomach, her frustration, her pain, and cleanse her, leave her a bloated corpse tumbling in the currents of her own anguish.

e filled her bath with cold water, gathered all her favourite photographs and cellotaped them over the tiles.

She left a note on the table. 'I'm going to die with my friends.'

She took a razor blade from her washbag.

Later Valerie burst down the door and found her with her goldfish swimming in the red waters of death.

She was barely alive.

* * *

After the transfusion Valerie held her tighter than was possible, so tight that she felt her bones in her hands and she told her that she didn't know if she needed her or anyone else and Valerie said to her that it was all right that she loved her, that Brian loved her, that her mother loved her, that everyone loved her and she asked: 'Are ye sure?' And Valerie told her that she would get Brian no matter what, but she didn't care. She drifted away.

* * *

For days Valerie and Brian looked after her, breathing their care into her. He told her he would show her some trees, the strongest trees in Leinster, that they had had been blown about as saplings, that the wind and ice had made them stronger, that what had happened to her would make her bigger, that sometimes in your life you think the whole world is pitted against you but in fact it was merely reflecting your own weaknesses and she told him that she would be all right that she was new again, that she'd try to keep the faces of her family, of him and of herself out of her own mind.

* * *

November.

He rang.

They drove to Emo Court, a house built in the early 18th Century, where they strolled around the gardens through brown and yellow leaves, flushing them across their shoes.

Winter gripped the skin of huge beech trees. In the air there was silence, the great peace that only the country can bring. In the quiet when they stopped walking, they listened to the leaves drop and sprinkle over the dew grass.

All around them a blanket of brown-yellow hues, beech, elm, oak and chestnut. Pigeons knifed across the clear ice-blue sky in threes. They walked to a lake and heard the gaggle of restless duck, hiding in the reeds.

Everywhere the anticipation of great cold. They ambled to the great house, its dome a memory of another age, two hundred years of history stored in granite and all around the gardens were statues carved with care and precision.

The music of the leaves dribbling from the oaks, the voice of hushed wind blowing the trees bare, the soft crestfallen branches cut against a chill crisp sky.

They strolled arm in arm, knowing that their season had ended also.

That day she wore the black dress she'd worn on the day of her father's funeral.

He told her about the cedars of Lebanon with their wide spreading branches, that they had been hewed by the servants of Hiram for Solomon's temple, about the great forests of North Africa which had supplied Ancient Rome with its cedar. She laughed at his knowledge. He told her again about the Book of Kells, its illustrations and its fugitive journeys around Ireland.

That day she looked into the face of this man and she loved him beyond reason. She had never felt in all the time that they had been so together, so close. Yet that day he never went near her.

He pulled out a blanket, some wine, two glasses and some

bread and cheese and they sat under the trees with the whisper of their memories blowing around them. He fetched the antique phonograph from the car and played some of the 78's. Mario Lanza, Richard Tauber, Nelson Eddie.

They looked into each others faces for all the world a trapped audience beached on a deserted island and when the light began to fail he put on McCormack singing 'Kiss me, my sweet' and tiny tears ran down her face.

He took her back to Dublin and outside her flat he held her tight, so tight that she knew inside that she'd lost someone, his hug felt to her like the desperate clutchings of a final farewell.

* * *

December.

Westland Row. It rained, white rain that needled down sheets of water. Trains lined up and cooing pigeons glided and flapped, sheltering from the storm .

He waited and sipped his coffee. In the corner of the restaurant there was a water boiler and in a glass display cabinet there were wrapped sandwiches. All about were small tables and chairs.

Outside Jenny passed with her suitcase and bags. She saw him, and he saw her. She stood hesitantly but after some moments made her way over. He stood up and greeted her. After some time she cut through the tension.

'How' ye doin'?' she asked.

He sat down.

'Valerie rang early this morning. She told me you were going,' he said.

She put all her bags down and pulled up a chair opposite him. She looked at a nun nearby, dipping a teabag in and out of a polystyrene cup.

'Can I get you some coffee, an espresso maybe?' he asked.

'Thanks,' she replied.

He went over to the food counter and moments later returned with a small coffee and put it down.

'How are ye? How ye doin'?' she asked again.

He nodded his head and raised one hand as if to say everything was so-so. There was a long pause.

She stirred sugar into her cup and watched him, her eyes full of gentleness, his eyes also.

'What's happenin'?'

She looked into him questioning.

'I came to say good-bye, that's all.'

'Why didn't ye call me? Ring me? Somethin', anythin', I didn't know what had happened to ye, I was so worried, are ye okay? I wanted to thank ye for the day at Emo and helpin' me to come back.'

He nodded looking into her eyes.

They stared into each other. 'Why does everythin' have to end? Can't we just go on? Why now? What am I goin' to do? I don't want to go to Belfast again, I want Dublin, I want yeu.'

He was silent looking at her, chewing the inside of his lip. She continued.

'What's happenin'? We can't leave it like this, talk to me, say something, ye said we could be friends, at least can we be friends? Brian!' she pleaded.

'It doesn't matter anymore.' he said.

'Ye don't understand, I love ye, yer inside me, ye keep me goin', ye've been good for me, Brian please talk to me, talk to me, at least talk to me,' she said in a raised voice.

'Cool it!' he said. 'We've been through this a thousand times.'

'Fuck them, I don't care what they think ... I don't care what anyone thinks anymore'.

After some moments, 'I'm sorry, I can't help myself, I didn't mean that, please can we be friends? At least let me write, somethin', anythin'.'

Her eyes watered up, she was cut up bad. They looked into each other. An announcement came over the speaker system.

'Ye remember how ye used to tell me about the Book of Kells?'.

He nodded.

'Do ye really dance with Ciara, that's lovely, that's really lovely, I'm so happy for her, she's really beautiful, ye know, yer so lucky with the children and yer work.'

She tried hard to stop herself from crying, some time passed. He bit into his gum. There was much love there.

'Ye told me someone was goin' to get hurt, ye were right, I should have listened to ye, ye've been so kind. Yer a good man, I'm sorry about the letters.'

'It's okay, I'm not good ... it's better this way...we've made a mistake,' he said

Jenny like a coil springing open shouted, 'No, it's not better, it wasn't a mistake. I've given ye so much love and everythin', why do ye have to be cruel? Why? Why? Why is it over? I love ye Brian O'Neill. Why can't ye handle two women? Why? Why?'

At the table behind them a nun got up and shuffled out.

'Stop it, cool it,' he said.

There was silence. She buried her head in her hands sobbing.

'Why does it have to end like this? Ye should have enough courage for both of us, ye've courage for everything else, why can't ye let me stay? There's nothin' for me in Belfast, ye know that, nothin'.'

'Jenny, I'm not the one sending you home, look, either way it's over, it's over in Belfast and it's over in Dublin.'

She opened a sachet of sugar, poured it into her coffee and breathed in deeply.

'I hate sugar, I don't know why I take it, I'll give it up, I know ye used to go on about sugar, I'll give it up.'

She lifted her head and looked into his eyes and the tears welling up. He watched her with big pain on his face.

She said, 'Ye keep going to yer Mass and sayin' yer prayers

and the dancin' and everythin' and, and ... everythin'.... and ...'

The final announcement was made for her train, only the two of them left sitting in the cafeteria.

'I'm sorry, I don't want to cry, I'm sorry, I don't mean it, I'll be strong like yeu, yer strong.'

She leaned over to get her bags and stood up.

'I'd better leave, ye know,' she said.

She looked into his face.

'Kiss me, Brian.'

'No, no kisses.'

'Oh Brian, just one kiss.'

Her face swollen up, distorted, crumpled up like a newborn child.

'Just one little one,' she pleaded.

'No.'

'No ... exactly ... I know ... ye know ... exactly.' It all came out anguished and distorted.

She picked up her bags and walked slowly to the door of the coffee shop. In the background an engine revved up high. She turned around and stared at him. She knew he was with her. He didn't move. She turned her back and left. He waited for some moments, looking at her empty coffee cup, the lipstick around the edges and the sugar all over the table. She disappeared from his view and he lifted the cup up to his lips, his hands shaking so much that the coffee spilled out. He put the cup down. Through the water in his eyes he watched the pigeons. He stared at one pigeon, concentrating hard on it till it flew out of his sight into the winter grey, into the rain.

* * *

SPRING

April.

The first week of Lent.

He took a train to Roscrea Abbey, a monastery set in the hills of Tipperary.

To flee from the torture of his passion, to work it out, to run with reason, to celebrate wisdom through prayer, to breathe easy, to escape his madness and live with the disciples of Christ, to ask for penance to appease the moral courts, to come to terms with his conscience.

He rose at five and watched the monks sing into the rafters of the church and the portals of heaven. For the first two to three days he seemed slow to touch on his conscience. Slow to feel the pulse of his folly during those lost months of the previous Summer. Each evening before Vespers he went to the side-chapel of St Joseph, where on the altar a solitary candle burned beside the purple-covered tabernacle. He prayed to the simple wooden cross on the wall, listening to the silence and the blood racing through his head and the voice of that girl trying to rekindle something inside him.

In the church the monks assembled robed and obedient to sing out the prayers of penance and suffering.

'In Qua reflorent omnia,
Laetemur in hoc ad tuam,
Per hanc reducti gratiam
Te rerum universitas.'

They raised and lowered their missals as they chorused the psalms. The season of Lent. The time of incense and blessed water.

'Kyrie Eléison, Christi Eléison, Kyrie Eléison.'

One of the brothers met him. They strolled around the grounds, through the rhododendrons and the maples up to the big gate.

The brother said, 'You suffer, you have no need. You must remember Christ forgives everything, nobody can ever understand the dimensions of His forgiveness ... Remember He is the same as us in everything but sin'.

'I've brought my problems on myself.'

The priest laughed.

'Remember the Gospel, last week the mountain, the Devil ... temptation ... You can solve those problems by yourself. God has given you the strength to do it, you know the right thing to do and you must act, otherwise your conscience will destroy you and you will destroy yourself ... You must remember a man must confront the thing he fears most.'

It made Brian think ... think about what he'd done to others and himself.

But it was on the Sunday of that week that he discovered conviction, the conviction of virtue, the conviction of revelation. When the bells rang out for Sunday Mass, each peel gave this man enlightenment and resolve. On that day he faced the stone altar stark and true, the brothers at each side of it in black robes and the ordained monks in white behind it. After receiving the host he was offered the heavy chalice and sipped sweet wine from the warm silver.

Through the darkness of his turmoil and his guilt, came a new light, as though he had discovered through his faith the intent, purpose and determination to scrape away the memory of that girl from the canvas of his mind.

* * *

It was the week before Easter. Ciara was in the kitchen sitting at the table. She painted faces onto hard-boiled eggs to hide in the garden on Easter Sunday.

She thought that it seemed to have all changed. Before there had been so many lonely times that even in the last three months she reckoned she was losing her mind, she had been sure that there had been something fundamentally wrong with their marriage. She had almost become crippled by his silence and yet there was his appetite for her physically which transcended all the questions.

She remembered one of her friends saying that when they

didn't want to do it, make love, it was over.

It had been a bad time for her. Before Christmas there had been the inexplicable phone calls and the strange hairs on a shirt that she'd found tossed away in a corner of his cupboard. There had been his distance, the way he seemed to float away as she talked to him, lost in a daze of distraction. There had been his hasty departures even when she knew that there was nowhere for him to go, his pathetic excuses and the smell of drink from him when he returned home hours later.

She sat there at the kitchen table with her brush and her tin of water colours and the hard-boiled eggs. She smiled at it all because now he seemed to have settled into her again. Her man. She made herself some tea and as she stirred the sugar about she thought to herself, how she used let him go, go anywhere as though deep down she knew that he must return, that her silence was maybe her greatest strength, the knowing that if she let him leave he would, like a dog who knows his home, always come back to her.

Since his trip to the country, to the monastery, he had mellowed. She felt he had come to terms with himself, had found some deep peace, that maybe his inner restlessness had disappeared in the mumblings of some mystic prayer.

She felt that the entire atmosphere in the house had been transformed. Before, they seemed to snap at each other, now, all was tranquillity and balance and a new harmony had settled over them.

She got up and made herself a sandwich, thinking how she had wanted to confront him on so many occasions but that would have required courage, courage to put it to him, courage to make him face the screaming inquisition that she had seen many times on TV ... But how it had all seemed to change. She felt as though their love was invincible.

She reflected back to her loneliness the previous autumn as she watched the light dying over Dublin Bay. She thanked God for her own patience.

He had time for her and the children, driving them all to Wicklow, to Dunmore East to watch the trawlers coming in, to Waterford where he told them stories about the Viking settlements and their surrender to Strongbow and the Normans.

That Lent he had inexplicably brought the bubble of happiness back to all of them, her respect for him had grown and they were going to Mass again. The family together.

Yet four nights later she awoke to the crash of thunder outside, not finding him in bed she ran downstairs. The back door was open and he was out in the middle of the garden, loaded with booze, the rain pouring down over him, over his hair, his face and his arms. He stared through her as though she was an apparition and she knew that the rain was bringing something back to him that night, the memory of it dragging him down again into the theatre of his own depression.

She went over to him and held him and held him tight.

'My Baby, my baby I love you, I'm here for you', she said.
She said: 'Let it go.'
She said: 'Let it go.'
She said: 'Let it go.'

She never mentioned that night to him again, knowing that she had seen the last remnants of his crisis being washed away.

She went to bed and cursed the rain.

* * *

Clouds dissipated.

It was a beautiful day and the sun came out hard and sharp bathing everyone in Spring and hope. On that Easter Sunday morning Ciara turned to her husband.

'Brian, the eggs are in that basket over there, the paint has dried out, make sure you hide them in good places, last year it was too easy.'

'Yeah okay, I'll camouflage them, they'll never find them, don't worry.'

He went to the back garden with a basket full of painted eggs and hid them, he called the children, they rushed out. Michael wasn't sure what it was all about, he took his son by the hand and brought him around a flower pot.

'What's that Michael?' he asked, pointing to one of the eggs lodged underneath the pot.

Michael didn't see it.

'Look there,' he insisted.

Michael touched the egg, picking it up in his fingers, looked at it and lifted it up in the air like a trophy.

'Look I found one, a red one, and it's got teeth.'

'I'll keep that Michael, you go find another one.'

'I've got one, I've got one!' Eileen screamed.

'Is there another one?' Michael asked.

'Yes darling, of course there's another one, there's loads of them.'

Eileen came over to him.

'Daddy, Daddy, give us a clue.'

'Well,' he said, 'I see a tree.'

Eileen went over and looked around the tree.

'Warmer, warmer, colder, warmer,' he said.

Eileen shouted, 'Daddy look I found another one, another one.'

Michael lifted his eyes up to him.

'Daddy?' he asked 'Where did you hide the big ones, the big chocolate ones'.

'We'll get them later,' he answered.

'Do you promise, the big chocolate ones?'

The children ran round and round the garden, the smell of fat coming from the lamb and potatoes roasting in the oven, the clump of fresh mint on the kitchen table, the peas boiling, the home-made icecream and the bottle of wine open, breathing. All about that house, family, happiness and love.

Resurrection.

Later in bed he scratched her back, the way she liked it and she had her fingers clenched tight in a ball and he watched her hand slowly open into the cradle of trust.

* * *

Jenny gained admission to Queen's University in Belfast and lived behind metal doors with her mother and her sister in Dundonald, East Belfast.

These were difficult times for her. She had no emotional or financial resources left. Wallace used the house to stay over, moving undercover between his own home in Ahoghill in Antrim and the house in Dundonald.

From being in a situation in Dublin where she had complete autonomy over her life, she now found herself under the wing of her mother once again and the ever present threat of Wallace terrified her. She attended evening lectures in Queen's and arrived home like an adolescent to be met by people who treated her like a child. She was given no respect. The worst of it all was that she had lost her confidence.

Where she had been free in Dublin to do as she wished, now her mother had become her jailer and her mother's wrath the rattle of keys and she couldn't find the courage inside herself to leave them. Her resentment grew. She swore that Wallace was having her watched and sometimes couldn't explain the deep feelings of fear that ran through her when he was in the house with his tattoos and his dancing eyes and his hours watching football videos of Glasgow Rangers.

Was this the punishment she must take for her love?

There were times when she locked herself away in her bedroom in order to crowd her imagination with memories of her time in Dublin, into a kind of hypnosis in which she felt she had become automatic, possessed.

She gazed at her bare walls, her mind filling with pictures, Dublin, the flat, the walk, the meals, the laughter, the jealousy, the rows, the lovemaking, his cigars, her fevered possessiveness, the pubs, Emo.

Every night after returning home from her lectures, she went to her room and resorted to dreams of her past, of those months in Dublin where she had come alive. Sometimes her mind slipped into the wildest state of hypotheses, crossing between truths and untruths, avoiding the reality of the present.

She fantasised about her lover, his smile, his wife, his children, she imagined having her own babies with him. Sometimes she lay on her bed and looked at all the cardboard boxes filled with her belongings, her collection, her life.

She wished she'd taken a photograph to help bring his face into her.

She thought how she'd love to let him smother her again with his kisses and his wildness and his crush for her. Deep down she knew that her feelings for him were real and strong, that in some way he must respond to them. He must react to the intensity of her yearning, let the melody of their obsession nurture the orchestra of uncontrollable emotions and let the symphony of illusion come crashing down through reality and bring him back to her.

Day after day in the confines of her imprisonment, unprotected from the disorder of her imaginings, she craved the past like a vulture clawing at the entrails of some slaughter returning time and time again to nourish her solitude.

In that bedroom illusion remained illusion, her mental anguish tortured her and she grew quiet, frail and introspective.

She lost her appetite. She imagined the cancer returning.

Seven months passed, her body became fragile and distorted, her hips lost their natural roundness, her stomach vacuumed in, her bottom lost its subtlety, her neck became thin and frail. The more her mother insisted, the less she cared, she wanted the rain and the rain had stopped.

Then she took up an invitation to go to Dublin for a football match.

WINTER

November.

The trees were bare. Their marriage was rich.

The bakery had thrived and they retained a cash surplus. When a hotel on the sea-front in Bray was put on the market, Frank and himself negotiated for it. The offer was accepted. Using outside equity and their own resources they secured the building. It was a good deal that gave these two men a night-club turning over a half a million a year.

They renovated and extended the club and little by little they refurbished the rest of the building, the bedrooms, the two lounges, the kitchen and the function rooms. The disco had a low ceiling, with a long bar running along the left side and a raised annex where customers dined. The tables gave a view over the dance floor behind which there was a smaller bar for the regular patrons. All around the dance floor were mirrors and lights, lights on the floor, lights set into the ceiling and lights recessed into the floor itself.

Frank concentrated on the bakery, taking nights off to come to the hotel to drink, chase and relax, in the main Brian had full autonomy over the club. He brought in live entertainment, local acts, bands, cabaret and soon it attracted a name. Each night there were four full-time security staff on duty, bar staff, a cloakroom attendant and a DJ.

Where the bakery had seemed to both partners to be a never ending battle with supplies, staff and cash-flow, the club was a far simpler operation.

* * *

That night it began to rain, slapping the streets, the sea with water, the kind of rain that would freeze over, that would river out into sheets of danger, the kind of rain that stayed over, settled, that heralded the curse of a long winter. They got a call, there was trouble at the side door of the hotel. Brian made his way over and opened the door, there was a group of men waiting to gain admission. The doorman explained that the men, Northern Irish football supporters, wanted to get access without going around to the front door where they'd have to pay.

'Look boys', he said, 'the night-club is separate from the hotel, you're all staying in the hotel, right? Well, come round to the front door, we'll charge you two quid, alright, happy?'.

One of the men went over to the doorman and whispered something in his ear. He saw the threat.

Brian asked, 'What's the problem? What did you say there?'

'I said nothin'.'

'The doorman looked at him.

'He said he was going to blow my fuckin' head off, Mr O'Neill.'

'Is that right? What's the problem with you guys? Why don't you learn some manners?'

Then he looked at them.

'None of you are going in, not tonight, not any night, nobody's going to make threats here and you're checking out of the hotel right now.'

'What are ye talkin' about? We did nothin'.'

'Look, you're out!'

He glanced over to the receptionist.

'Check them out.'

'Yes Mr O'Neill.'

He moved to the man that had made the threat, pointing into his chest.

'Get your bags, you've ten minutes!' he said angrily.

'Jesus Christ, we're meetin' our women here, c'mon be fair.'

'Out, end of story!' he repeated.

Two bouncers came into the hall. Standing off, the two groups stared at each other. The supporters slowly backed off and went up the staircase. Brian looked to the receptionist.

'If they're not out in ten minutes I want to know.'

'What will I charge them?' she asked, concerned.
'Nothing.'
One of the men turned to him.
'Where will we go at this hour?'
'That's not my problem, you can camp out in Lansdowne Road for all I care.'
One of the doormen opened the door.
'You're a fuckin' Nationalist!' he said.
He turned to him and replied, 'Listen, my only cause is my pocket, go on inside and keep an eye on the floor.'

* * *

The doorman watched the girls come in.
'Are you with the football guys?'
One of them, a plump girl, with a head-scarf looked up.
'Yeah, we're meeting our friends inside.'
'They've gone.' The doorman told her.
'Gone. Where?'
'I'm sorry love, they're barred.' the doorman said.
One of them approached him.
'Who barred them? They're with us, for Jesus sake, we're only here for the game.'
'Mr O'Neill owns the place, he's the boss. If you want to, you can sort it out with him, but you can't go in without paying, simple.'
She stepped forward. Jenny. She closed down an umbrella.
'Wait a sec, how ye doin? What's this guy's first name?'
'Brian. Brian O'Neill.'
'Did he ever sell cakes, did he have a bakery?'
'Yeah that's it.' the doorman said.
She glanced at her friend.

* * *

Robert Palmer sang in the background. Frank sat in the restaurant with a girl, she was tall, thin with a big lipstick mouth.

Jenny walked in and approached his table.

'Hello Frank' she said. 'How ye doin?'

Frank's eyes widened but after some time he composed himself.

'What are you doing here?' he stood up. 'Christ, you're thin!'

'I came for the match ... some people from college.'

He touched the ice-bucket beside him and took the wine out.

'Would you like some?'

'No thanks, my friend's gone to get some drinks.'

'Has he seen you? Did you know we were here?'

'No.'

'No what?'

'No that's all.'

'Jenny this isn't good, this isn't good, you can't stay here, this is bad for everyone. Jesus Christ! This is a fucking disaster.'

'Frank, is he here?' she bent forward.

'No, I, yes he is, please Jenny you're, you're jinxed.'

Frank looked behind her at a girl coming towards them. Her friend, arrived with two pints of Guinness, she put them on a table .

'This is Deborah,' Jenny said.

'Hello Deborah, I'm Frank.'

He extended his hand politely but the face was serious.

'Look I'll talk to you in a minute, excuse me,' he said.

He turned, walked upstairs to the office and opened the door.

'She's here.' he said.

'Who?' Brian asked.

'Your friend "exactly".'

'Who are you talking about?'

'Remember "ye know ... ye know, ye know, exactly, exactly".'

'Shit Frank, what are you saying ... I'm busy.'

'She's here, she's in the night-club, Jenny, that girl you were with last year, the one who did your head in.'

Brian stood up.

Frank said, 'Don't tell me I didn't warn you,' and bent towards him. 'Brian listen to me, that girl is all flares and short-lived, don't go back, I'm tellin' you your wife is like a vein of gold, don't go back, please ... you know what it did to you, the last time.'

He closed the door.

Brian waited a moment, bit his lip and walked out after him. Frank went to his table and sat down. Brian walked towards the girl and came in close, she looked up to him.

'How ye doin?'

For a time they looked at each other without words.

'Ye haven't changed.' she said.

He sat down.

'You look thinner, a lot thinner,' he said.

She blushed, embarrassed.

'This is a nice wee place, yer doing well, I'm glad.' she replied.

A waitress arrived.

'Would you like a drink Mr O'Neill?'

'Paddy ... large,' he replied.

They didn't talk, Madonna sang in the background, the dance floor filled, strobe lights pinpointed the dancers, smoke filled the floor.

'How's Belfast?'

'Belfast is Belfast, roadblocks, body searches, more roadblocks, ye know yerself.'

Frank cut in.

'I'll see you in a minute.'

He got his girl and went over to the bar and watched them, muttering,'I don't like it, I don't like it at all.'

'Are you staying down here?' Brian asked.

'Just tonight and tomorrow, I'm here for the game.'

'Since when were you into football?'

She grimaced, surprised by his cynicism but her heart was thumping, she didn't know what to do with her hands which felt like two spades, she wondered whether her hair, her make-up, her teeth were right. He stood up.

'I've got to go.'

He pushed his chair in to the table.

'It was nice seeing you again.'

He extended his hand, walked out of the restaurant, opened the sidedoor and went into the hotel to drink.

* * *

Later – after they closed the club – he sat by one of the tables, watching the cleaners and listening to Barry White.

He couldn't understand why the whiskey didn't burn away the knot in his stomach, why the control he'd spent so long nourishing hung on a tightrope of uncertainty. And he turned around and like a ghost she walked towards him.

'Can I join ye?'

'I thought you'd left.'

'Ye don't have to talk to me like that.'

'I forgot, I have to be nice. How, ah, never mind, where are you staying?'

'Greystones.'

He moved to the bar, got a bottle of whiskey and put it on the table. She waited until he poured some.

'How ye doin' Brian? I mean, really how ye doin'?'

She was close, he didn't react.

'I'm fine, this is different, I'm doing alright. Look Jenny, it's ....'

He turned to face her. There was a protracted silence. He looked at her reflection in the mirrors, the hair seemed different to him.

'Brian, let me inside ye, I'm only here for one night.'

'I can't, I'm sorry, why did you come back, did you think,

did you know I was here? Jesus .... Jenny, listen to me, I fell in love with you, but it's over, it's dead'.

'We were goin' to go up the road.' she slurred.

'Have you been drinking?' he asked.

She smiled and lit a cigarette.

'I was only goin' to stay for the night, they ... '

'Who are they?'

'My mother...and ye know.'

'Oh that shit, I forgot, won't they miss you?'

'They watch me like a hawk.'

'I can imagine' he said indifferently. 'Is she still beating you up?'

She didn't answer.

'You've got to stand up for yourself. I thought you would have grown out of that by now,' he said.

She looked into his eyes. The eyes of the man. His mouth, his teeth, but his smile was hard towards her. She felt nervous, but inside a creeping emptiness. He had changed.

'I don't want to talk about the past, I'm glad I saw ye again, I can't tell ye what it's been like, I just am glad that I've seen ye again, there was so much goin' on in my head, I'm glad, that's all.'

'You're not the only one.' he replied.

'Have ye time tonight, time to talk?'

'No, if I give you tonight ...'

There was a long silence. He continued.

'I'll give you everything I've got left.'

She pulled on her cigarette. He waved for the cleaner to leave the room.

'Ye know' she said, 'there hasn't been a day ...', she paused, 'I haven't thought about us.'

He stood up.

'Listen, you can't walk in here expecting things to be the same, it's not like that anymore, I've moved forward ... it was a mistake for both of us, you know that.'

She looked at him.

'Ye were always on a mission Brian, yeu and Frank, ye know.'

'I know a lot of things, and I know you shouldn't be here.'

He finished his whiskey.

'I'll bring you to Greystones.'

'Now!' she said surprised.

'Yeah, now.'

He stood up, she put her drink down and stood close to him.

'Brian.'

He didn't move, she touched the buttons on his shirt, fiddling with one of them turning it around and around and around, he didn't stop her.

'Are you clear?' he asked without moving or touching her.

'Yes.'

She tugged at her hair.

'It's real look, see.'

'I thought it was different,' he said.

'Exactly,' she said, like he'd heard it a million times before.

There was a noise outside, the sound of glass shattering. He moved away from her and ran towards the side door of the night-club.

'Fuckin' hell, what's that?'

He reached the door, two men in balaclavas ran in, one of them going straight for him, hitting him flat on the bridge of his nose.

'Who are you, what the fuck!' he shouted, but by the time he had it out, a man with a leather jacket had wrestled him to the ground. Brian momentarily got a foothold and swung out wild, connecting once but these men had done this before and they rained punches on him, one of them screaming:

'What did ye do that for ye little fuck?'

They held him, pinning him to the ground, hands over

his head, a third man entered wearing a balaclava, looking at Jenny with her silent scream.

'Jenny, Wallace is outside, he wants a wee word with ye.' Brian shouted.

'Jenny, you're going nowhere.'

One of the men hit him hard on the side of his head and a third man went over, kicked him and put a hand over his mouth.

The door sprang open. Wallace made his entrance. Wallace. Shaven. Height 5'8. Weight 200 pounds. Fit. Weather-beaten complexion. Small eyes. The eyes of death.

'Ye stay away from him, ye stay away, ye bastard, ye leave him alone, ye bastard.' she shouted, rushing towards Wallace. The man looked at her, grinning, a mouth full of broken teeth.

'Who do ye think yer talkin' to lassie.' he said. 'Did yer mother not warn ye about this, did she not mark yer card about this Fenian Fuck, ye get outside, she's waitin' for ye in the car.'

'Ye bastard, I'm going nowhere with ye.'

'Yer goin' outside.'

He grabbed her by the arm, one hand fastened over her mouth and marched her out. In the background coming out of speakers, Barry White:

> '... I've found what the world is searchin' for,
> right, right here,
> never going to give you up,
> I'm never goin' to quit.'

Brian was sprawled on the metal dance floor, surrounded by men in balaclavas. Wallace returned with a large black holdall. He pulled up a chair, sat down, took a cigarette from a pack in his top pocket and lit it with a Zippo lighter, his eyes never once leaving Brian's face. He sat back and sucked deep drags. The tip of the cigarette glowed as he rocked his head.

'Is that wee Barry I'm listenin' to, I like wee Barry White,' he said.

The song finished. He stood up, took off his jacket showing his tattoos, pulled a sledgehammer from the holdall, sat back in the chair and took a cloth from his pocket. He began to clean the iron head.

'Do ye know what this is, ye filthy Taig', he said smiling malevolently.

'Sit him up against the pillar', he directed the others.

The men in balaclavas dragged him over and propped him against a mirrored pillar.

'I like my students to learn, ye know, watch and learn jus' like school, that's good, I like that ... jus' like school.'

He sucked on a cigarette, his eyes on Brian as he turned the head of the sledgehammer over in his lap. He took the cigarette from his mouth, looked intently at the tip and in one movement brought the cigarette down onto the skin of his own left hand, burning it without flinching until the skin seared and singed. He put the sledgehammer down and reached into the holdall, pulled out a Browning and a handful of bullets and began slotting them into the magazine. Under his breath he murmured, 'Fuckin' Taig!'

'Ye've never suffered, have ye' ... I fuckin' suffer, everyday, just like that, I fuckin' suffer but I can take it, what about ye.'

He chuckled, staring at the wound on his hand.

'Do ye like my tattoos? Ye see that one son, the red hand, ye see these letters there U.Y.M. Do ye know what that means, son? Ulster Young Militant, what do ye think of my Union Jack? Ye Fenian fuck!'

He pulled open his shirt.

'Turn up the lights in here lads till I show this Taig my wee gallery.'

One of the men went over to the DJ's box and hit a switch. Lights filled the room as Wallace flexed his muscles. The flag was emblazoned across his back, in it's centre a bull mastiff with a helmet in which was painted the red hand.

He moved his shoulders.

'Ye like that son? Do ye see this one?'

He pointed to his left shoulder, another red hand.

'Do ye like it? This here is a picture here of the B Specials.'

On his arm a man in a black uniform, and on his neck and across his chest, tattoos, black with ink and design. He closed over his unbuttoned shirt and waved the gun.

'This one is real good for business, heh, heh, heh, what about ye, real stopping power here, heh, heh. This, my friend, is business. Ye Fenian Fuck!'

He put lettered fingers around the trigger, pointed the gun at one of the mirrored walls and squeezed. In an echoing explosion the wall shattered, splintering glass cascaded onto the floor. He pointed the gun at another wall and pulled the trigger, more glass shattered under the impact of bullets. He reloaded the gun and emptied the magazine into the bar. Bottles, glasses, mirrors exploded and cordite smoked out filling the room.

He laughed, 'I hope yer cleaners are comin' in early son.'

He began to fire into the DJ's box, it disintegrated into fragments of glass and wood.

'Ye see mister ladies' man, I'm really a song and dance man myself, but really most of all I like peace and quiet so that I can watch football, ye know what I'm sayin'.'

Two of the men holding Brian laughed, showing white teeth in the slot of their balaclavas.

'Now that's the wee music sorted out,' he said.

He put the gun down on the floor and picked up the sledgehammer.

'Ye see son, yer nothin', nothin'.'

Wallace stood up.

'C'mon take his pants off, be quick about it. I don't need fuckin' Fenian romeos.'

Terror filled Brian's eyes as one of the men held a firm grip over his mouth.

'Look son, ye better watch yerself, what's yer problem

with yer fuckin' dick, Fenian fuck, didn't we warn ye. Didn't we tell ye to keep yer distance?'

One of them shouted, 'he's fuckin' not listenin' to ye!'

'C'mon give him a hidin',' another demanded.

Wallace rubbed the head of the sledge hammer with a cloth.

'Get his fuckin' pants off quick.'

Brian's head moved from side to side. He tried to kick out. Wallace gazed on him and picked up the gun, he put it into Brian's mouth to show what he was about. Brian stopped struggling. They removed his pants. One of the men had his knee in his stomach, the other pulled his leg out and gripped his foot tight, turning it.

Wallace withdrew the gun, put it down lifted the sledgehammer over his shoulder and in an arc of violent rage brought it down onto Brian's knee. At the moment of impact, Brian's face contorted into wretched pain and he roared into the hands over his mouth. Bone came out through skin, his leg was shaking and split open, blood running over his shin and onto the floor.

'Didn't we tell ye to keep yer distance?' Wallace hissed. 'Didn't I even phone ye last year, but ye wouldn't fuckin' listen, ye Fenian Fuck, get the other leg out. What about ye, what about ye.' Brian's head moved from side to side, again Wallace lifted the sledgehammer. The side-door swung open. Jenny came in shouting.

'Leave him alone, leave him alone!' she charged at Wallace and sank her teeth into his arm.

'Jesus, ye bitch!' he shouted throwing her off over the broken glass.

'Get her out of here, get her into the car, get her fuckin' out of here!'

One of the men picked her up and threw her out. She yelled: 'Leave him alone, he's done nothin' to ye, he's done nothin, leave him alone.'

'C'mon,' said Wallace to the others, opening the holdall.

'Ye can count yerself lucky, ye needed a wee lesson, don't ye come near her again, right.' he shouted. 'Ye catch yerself on, do ye hear, catch yerself on,' he warned, his two fingers to his temple. Each of the men spat, hitting him with phlegm and left. The door closed. Brian couldn't move, the consciousness of pain transgressing all reality, becoming the focus of his existence. Nothing could superimpose over it. It was the centre of his being, the source of everything and beyond.

He lay on the night-club floor trying to breathe, the piercing ache racking through his body.

* * *

The two detectives were with her in the house. One of them leaned against a wall.

'I knew something had happened', Ciara said. 'I knew something was wrong, I couldn't sleep, I felt it, I was so sure something had happened, I knew it, I knew something terrible had happened.'

The detective blew his nose, looked at his partner and stared back at her.

'You'll want to tell your husband that we're taking the matter very seriously and we want questions answered.'

Ciara looked at them.

'I knew something was going to happen in that place, I knew it, I could feel it in my bones.'

The detective looked into her face.

'Mrs O'Neill, if your husband isn't going to help us with our enquiries, we can't proceed, we need names!'

'I don't know. I don't know ... you understand ... I don't know why this has happened. Who did this to my husband? Why ....? What's happening? ... Why is it raining like this?'

The detective stared blankly at her.

'We'll call the hospital tomorrow, you have a word with him, we want these people, we want names, your husband

knows. He knows,' he said. 'You must talk to him.'
'I don't understand. I don't understand any of this!'
'Look Mrs O'Neill, we'll leave it with you.'
They left. Eileen came in.
'Mummy what did they want.'
'It's nothing, nothing at all.' she said biting her lip.
She went into the kitchen and broke down crying, the terrifying spectacle of her man, a victim of a kind of crime that she couldn't understand. That night she slept with Eileen on one side and Michael on the other. In the morning she awoke to find that she was lying in a pool of warm water, to discover it was her own sweat.

* * *

Two weeks later. They were in the kitchen. He rested against his crutch. He'd become accustomed to the angle, ensuring that the rubber at the bottom was well set against the ground.
'What's the matter with you?' Ciara asked. 'Why don't you talk to me? God I can't stand the tension anymore, you've got to cut it out, we've got to discuss what's happening.'
She moved to the back-door.
'Not now Ciara, not now.'
'I feel as though I'm losing you again, it's like since you've come out of the hospital that I don't exist inside you, you're cold.'
'Ciara.'
He limped towards her.
'Ciara, I love you, I have huge feelings for you, when this thing happened I closed up, it's, I can't explain it.'
She cried out, 'I have feelings too and you're destroying them!'
He turned his back and tried to sit.
She continued, 'It's as if you're trying to cut me away, I

know you, I know the way you are, we have to talk, Brian.'

Eileen walked in.

'Mummy, Mummy can you tie Michael's laces they're always opening, I can't do it.'

Michael shuffled in with one shoe in his hand, Brian took a chair, bent over, pulled on the boy's shoe and tied the black string. Ciara looked over at him.

'What I'm trying to tell you, what I'm trying to tell you is that ...'

She waited for him to finish tying Michael's laces.

'... Is that I'm not going back to last year, you must believe what I'm saying, I'm adamant about it. I'm upset Brian. I don't understand what's going on, but I'm not going back to last year, Brian'.

He went over to the boiling kettle, switched it off and made tea.

She looked into him, 'What's going on, look at me Brian, you've got to tell me, are you paying protection?'

He turned.

'Don't be fuckin' mad!'

He sipped tea.

'This is something I need to sort out on my own.'

'You know you're in over your head, who did this to you?

'I told you, we had trouble in the night-club that's all, and that's it.'

'Go on.'

'We barred someone, he waited for me, he had a wheel brace.'

He sat down.

'I know you Brian and I know when you're telling the truth, and you're lying.'

'That's the truth.'

'You're lying, I know you're lying, lying, lying, lying.'

She stirred the teaspoon around in the cup. After a time she said, 'I wish you had told the police something, anything, I didn't want to talk about it while you were in hospital, I wish you'd never got into that scene, I hate nightclubs, Brian, please tell me, tell me what happened'.

'Listen, this is the business I've got myself into, it's the way it is, sometimes things happen, I've got to sort it out myself.'

He avoided her eyes.

'Can't you see I'm a human being, I'm your wife.' she pleaded, leaning over the table and burying her head in her hands.

'You've gone all quiet, I wish, I wish I had the old Brian back.'

'You'll get me back, you've just got to hang in there.'

He moved to her and said 'You've got to hang in with me, we've got to ride this out together'.

She put her arms around his waist.

'Oh Brian, hang onto me, help me protect you from yourself, I'm so afraid, I've seen you like this before, I don't understand, the children need you.'

Her eyes filled with tears.

'Jesus, baby!' he said.

'I trust you so much, I don't ever want to lose you,' she said.

She rubbed his arm.

'Please Brian ... Please.'

He let his crutch go and put his hands through her hair as she sobbed.

'You've got me baby, you've got me.'

He looked through the kitchen window at the children playing outside, happy and carefree. The children he'd created.

* * *

December.

She had felt that Christmas was going to be good for all of them but since the beating, everything had transformed, he had changed. Again she had begun to witness the tormented silences and her marriage undermined as though the previous months had been nothing but a dream, a canvas on which some illusionist had sprayed colours as though all the time they had been going down a one-way street and only now she discovered that there was absolutely no way out.

She must face the truth, what had happened to her husband, what was happening to him, was his silence an admission of some guilt or was he trying to protect her from the truth of violence and in the pit of her stomach she knew that there was something terribly, terribly wrong, she knew that her man was being taken away by the power of some voice, some voice that had never spoken to her and she felt so alone with her children, her anxiety and her desperate need for the truth.

* * *

Through a drizzle the sun streamed its peach evening light into the room.

She made up her shopping list and left him in the kitchen. The phone rang and Brian picked it up.

'This is Val, Val, Valerie, Jenny's friend.'

'Yeah I know you Valerie, I know you, what is it?'

'Can you talk?'

'Yeah.'

'It's Jenny, she's overdosed.'

'She's what?'

'She's overdosed, she's in hospital, I came back to my flat, she was in the toilet.'

'Your ecstasy pills!' he demanded.

'I don't know how she found them.'

'Jesus Christ. I knew it, you and 'E', has she been staying with you? ... is she okay?'

He held the phone away from him, making a face of anger

and brought the receiver back to his ear.
'What?'
'Is she alive?'
'I don't know, the ambulance took her away, yes she, I think so, she's in some hospital, I had to tell her mother, she's suicidal Brian, somebody's got to do something.'
'Yeah, like giving her fuckin' E tablets.'
'Brian, she's bad.'
'Have they pumped her ... is she conscious?'
'I know nothing nothing. Help me, help her, you're the only one ... I can't talk to her.'
'Give me your number.'
He grabbed a pen and wrote it.
'She told me what happened, are you okay, I mean, listen, they're insane, I mean her mother and that guy.'
She was panicky.
'I don't know what they'll do to her, Brian, you've got to help!'
He looked out at the rain washing against the window, dripping from the skeleton branches of the trees in his back garden.
'Look I'll ring you, you stay there by the phone, I'm coming. I'll ring you on Saturday.' He remembered how Valerie had told him about her in the bath, her eyes barely open, the fish swimming in the bathwater.

* * *

Frank ordered drinks.
'I'm going to sort that bastard out.'
'You're mad Brian.'
'She overdosed.'
'How do you know'
'Her friend rang.'
'Not that dark-haired one ...Valerie ... she's a nutter.'
'She took a rake of ecstasy.'

'Stay away from her ... that girl makes you live on the edge ... is she alive?'

'Yeah, they pumped her out.'

'Then leave it.'

'It's not enough.'

'Brian, listen to me you're fuckin' mad getting involved again, look can't you see that you're playing back into her hands, it's just not right, look what you have at home, a beautiful wife who adores you ... two beautiful children. You've got to transfer your emotions into what's right, not this. Jesus, Brian, Ciara is your best friend, she's good for you, let that Jenny one sort out her own problems. Listen to me you're lucky to be alive, remember the railway crossing in Sandymount last year. Jesus – you're lucky that guy didn't shoot your brains out in the club, don't go looking for revenge, there's too many up there doing that already.'

'This isn't about revenge.'

'Yeah, well it certainly looks like it from where I'm sitting.'

Brian gulped Guinness.

'She'll do herself in Frank ... this is a suicide I'm not going to let happen ... I'd never live with myself.'

'Brian for Christ's sake, can't you see what you're getting yourself into, everything that girl does is a scream for help.'

Frank eyed him seriously. 'Look it's like this, you're reacting without thinking it out, there's enough paramilitaries up there who'll want to get him, mark my words, he'll be rubbed out, these people end up killing each other.

'I don't know Frank, all I know is this is the worst thing that could have happened, it's worse, she's lost hope'.

'Listen Brian, she isn't going to kill herself and you don't want to get involved with these people, OK?'

Brian reacted, 'You don't understand, do you.'

Frank slammed his pint down 'You'll be the one to get killed Brian ... is that what you want ... is it ... you want to fucking die? Come on, come on ... that's what you fucking want isn't it?' he said, raising his voice.

'I'm not sitting back on this one ... someone's got to do something.' Brian answered. He lifted his crutch and made for the door.

You're a fuckin' eejit.' Frank shouted.

Brian picked up his crutch and turned to him.

'Keep an eye on her.'

'You're fuckin mad, can't you let sleeping dogs lie.'

Brian looked at him and walked alone into the carpark.

* * *

On Saturday morning he climbed out of bed, put on his pants, his shirt and his shoes. He went into the bathroom and shaved, his eyes on his eyes in the mirror. When he finished he washed the razor under the cold tap and put it into his pocket. He brushed his teeth and returned to the bedroom.

'I've got to go.'

He leaned over and kissed his wife.

'Oh, that's nice. You haven't kissed me in ages.'

She stretched, sat up and rubbed her face but she must have sensed his urgency.

'Brian, you never get up early on Saturday mornings. Where are you going?'

He reached down beside the bed for his crutch.

'Please, Brian, what are you doing?'

'Where I'm going you don't want to know.' he muttered.

'Brian, no, Brian, please, please tell me!'

She sat bolt upright in bed. He took a tie from a chair, put it around his neck and began to make the knot.

'Why are you not telling me, you're going to do something stupid, why are you doing this?'

He took his jacket and turned to her.

'Because darling...' he didn't finish.

'Brian!' she shouted.

But he was already out the door. At the top of the landing his son Michael looked at him.

'Are you going to make money today, Daddy?'

He picked him up.

'I am, darling, I am.'

'Will you bring it home?'

'I will, darling, I will.' He hugged his son and made his way down to the front door into the driveway and opened the door of the car. He heard her calling after him.

'Don't do it, Brian, let me drive you, please!'

She stood at the front door, a towel wrapped round her.

'I'm only going down the road', he said, 'I'll be grand, I'm going to have a look at some stuff for the night-club, go on inside.'

She came to the car door, her eyes on him, knowing he was lying.

'No Brian, no!' she shouted, her hands up to her mouth.

He drove away. She went back to the kitchen, made some coffee and sat at the table. She had a recurring thought about his death. She glanced at a photograph of him taken after Michael was born and she couldn't understand why he had changed so much. The face that looked back at her she didn't recognise.

* * *

He drove the car through Dundalk to the Newry checkpoint. The shadow of green misty rain groaning all over the country, sheeting the light with crystals of water. As the vapour-thin rain came down over the windscreen and the wipers moved from side to side, he reflected on his wife and Jenny, on all the times that it had rained.

* * *

Jenny
'My father used to tell me that I would always bring the rain with me.'

Ciara
'Sometimes when it rains, you get so impatient Brian, let it run over you, let it go, you've got to learn patience.'

Jenny
'This fuckin' rain, all my clothes are soakin', I always seem to be dryin' things, ye know, I've no heaters, Brian ye better start prayin' that it's goin' to stop. Since I've met ye, it's been rainin', it must be the worst summer ever, it's always so damp, I don't know how those traders downstairs stick it, my bones are always cold. I'm sick of this flat, I'm not an indoors type of person, if only the rain would go, why don't we make love or somethin'.'

Ciara
'Brian you see these coats you've got for the children, they're useless, can't they make coats that work, Brian the gutters are all blocked, God, I wish I could go out for a walk, to smell the air, just to feel it.'

Jenny
'My shoes are wet, my socks are wet, my feet are cold, everythin' I have is wet except my hair.'

Ciara
'All I do is shop and collect the children from school, ever since I married you, Brian, I just seem to be repeating my actions all the time, day in, day out. Brian remember, I qualified, I can be a doctor

anytime.'

Jenny

'Ye don't understand his violence, it's like ye don't want to understand it.'

Ciara

'I wish I could come with you, you know I love being with you maybe I could get my mother to baby-sit, we could go to Galway. That would be really nice to look at the rocks in Galway Bay and walk the beaches.'

Jenny

'Brian I don't want to be anything other than yer mistress, I'd never marry ye, I know I want love, well really, I want everythin', I want everythin' Brian, ye understand, but I'd never marry ye.'

Ciara

'I want to get out of the house, go somewhere, anywhere.'

Jenny

'I want a pint, Brian get us a wee pint, will ye?'

Ciara

'Could I have a gin and tonic please?'

Jenny

'I'd love a water bed, I'd love to have my birthday on a waterbed, just drink champagne and make love and watch ye smoke yer cigars.'

Ciara

'Don't you ever fix the creaks in this bed, I know

it's loud but I love the noise it makes.'

Jenny
'I love all kinds of music. Rap, techno, acid and heavy metal, but I suppose I really, really love Nirvana and the Doors.'

Ciara
'The Gypsy Kings are brilliant, Brian can we get away from this rain, go to Spain or Portugal, and dance in the sun.

Jenny
'I'm out of cigarettes, give us some money Brian while I get a wee packet of ciggys, wow, I think this is my second packet today, I'll have to cut back. I wish I could give them up, ye know.'

Ciara
'If you take up cigarettes Brian, I'm going to smoke as well, you smell disgusting, how would you like it if you woke up beside a chimney, it's not pleasant, that night-club is disgusting.'

Jenny
'Are ye sayin' that I can't cook, right I'll show ye and I won't buy it in this time and no meat, I never eat my friends.'

Ciara
'I've got some nice steaks for you, I think I'll grill them with some garlic, broccoli, asparagus and sour cream. Why don't you take a shower? It'll be ready for you when you come down.'

Jenny
'When yer not around all I seem to eat is noodles,

noodles and more noodles and I'm broke.

Ciara
'Eileen really misses you, she keeps asking where you are, you know Brian she notices how long you're gone, do you know something, Michael is now eight years old, do you realise that?'

Jenny
'This is stupid, so stupid, maybe I've been foolin' myself all along.'

Ciara
'Brian we need to spend more time together, you and me ... and I want a ring.'

Jenny
'Brian ye better buy me glasses since ye swallowed my lenses ... my eyes have got really sore.'

Ciara
'I've never watched so much TV, I could even draw the picture of the Virgin they have during the Angelus.'

Jenny
'My periods are really messy, I think I've got somethin' wrong with me, maybe it's the pill, there's so much blood and I'm always weepy, I feel so sick, I think I'll have another check up, I've just found a pill loose in my handbag.'

Ciara
'Brian, don't you come near me, don't you dare come near me.'

Jenny
'Where have ye been? Fuck ye.'

Ciara
Put the bins out.

Jenny
You're my king, my wee king.

Ciara
'Will you be late home Brian? please, Brian we never see you, the only time I see you is when you're asleep.'

Jenny
'It's never goin' to be over between us is it Brian, say it's never goin' to be over.'

Ciara
'Brian are you bored with me, is that it, are you, are you, tell me honestly are you?'

Jenny
'You have the same laugh as me Dad!'

Ciara
'The only time you're nice is when you're asleep!'

Jenny
'I can't understand how ye put up with my temper, I've only really lost it once, maybe twice, haven't I Brian, I mean, oh shit, Brian, it's not that bad is it?'

Ciara
'You know the sex seems to get better and better, I mean I really seem to be letting go, like I want your tongue, your cock, everything.'

Jenny
'In the beginnin' it was like ye were my boyfriend, after a while ye became my brother and in the end it's like ye've become my father, Jesus, ye'll end up being God lookin' at my tombstone .'

Ciara
'We haven't made love for weeks, you just seem to ignore me, am I too old, why are these wrinkles so big? I don't want to grow old. But I want to have more children and grandchildren and great grandchildren.'

Jenny
'I want fun, ye know F.U.N.' She spells it out.

Ciara
'Does Frank smoke?'
'Does Frank have a family?'
'Does Frank go out much?'
'Does Frank always wear those waistcoats?'
'He really turns me on.'

Jenny
'Havin' cancer makes ye value time, maybe that's why I'm all messed up, ye know.'

Ciara
'I hate the smell of donuts. Every time I'm with you you smell of burnt fat.'

Jenny
'This flat is full of the smell of cigars, I love it, even when ye've gone yer still here, ye know.'

Ciara
'You're coughing too much, I'm worried.'

Jenny
'I want to get a new wig.'

Ciara
'I want to get my hair done.'

Jenny
'I want to let my hair grow under my arms, my legs all over the place, the wee natural look, ye know, everywhere. All over.'

Ciara
'I've shaved really close and I mean everything.'

Jenny
'The way ye touch me, its so good, oh touch me, touch me there, yes there.'

Ciara
'I want to make all the moves, all the moves, let me, I said let me do it.'

Jenny
'Fuck me, lick me, look at me, watch me, kiss me, lick me, love me.'

Ciara
'Now take me now, oh yes, oh yes, fuck me good.'

Jenny
'Exactly, exactly, exactly. Yes, yes, yes!'

Ciara/Jenny
'Yes, oh yes, oh yes, oh yes!'
'FUCK ME, FUCK ME, FUCK ME!'

* * *

He switched on the radio and listened to the news, during the night a bomb had gone off under a landrover in Twinbrook, at least four soldiers were believed to be dead. He turned it off. It had taken him two hours to reach the border. He approached the checkpoint. On either side of him there was a concrete wall guiding his car into a confined space, a soldier stood behind a wire fence watching him. There were mounted cameras behind cages. Eyes peered out from a hole in a concrete look-out.

An R.U.C. policeman walked towards the car, a clipboard in his hands and told him to wind down the window. He heard the drone of a helicopter echoing high up over his head.

'Where are you going Sir?'

'Belfast, business.'

'How long will you be staying?'

He looked at the green uniform and the cap with its insignia. The policeman peered into the back of the car.

'A day, maybe two.' he said.

'Switch off your engine and open the boot please Sir? '

He climbed out and lifted the boot open, there was a box of paperwork that he had meant to bring over to his accountants. The man looked inside the box as a soldier moved near.

'Okay, Sir.'

He waved him on. Brian shook his head in disbelief at this theatre.

'Sorry, Sir?' said the policeman who had seen this.

'Nothing,' he replied.

The policeman walked around the car and read the registration into his mike.

'Your address, please Sir?'

He gave it. The policeman waited for confirmation and waved him on.

He was in the North. Place of sadness and war.

* * *

She'd been in Intensive Care in the Royal Victoria, locked into a drug-induced coma. For four days and nights the doctors had worked on her with pumps, oxygen and plasma. Now she sat upright in a bed with a bowl of jelly in her hands but she had no interest in it. She put the plate down and stared at the prints of the flowers in the folds of the curtains around the bed.

Her eyes had lost the magic shine, once mirroring her energies, now empty without life, containing the glaze and stare of someone in paralysis. On a steel table beside the bed there were oranges in a fruit basket and some unopened magazines. The previous day her mother had visited. She tried not to acknowledge her even when her mother bent down and said close into her ear, 'I came to see ye, because I want ye back with us. Back where ye belong'.

'Please go away. I'm never comin' back, never ... never ... never!'

And then she overheard her mother talking to one of the nurses. She had said, 'I want a good eye on her ... a good eye on her ... a good eye on her.'

She sat up and listened. She could hear the distinct sound of a motorbike outside with it's throttle wide open and it gave her the feeling of imprisonment, of being forever locked into a nightmare world of isolation, violence and hatred. The nurses tried to speak with her, she looked at them, without responding. She went to the bathroom with assistance. At times she held an orange and turned it over in her hands. At times she just lay there listening to the sounds of life.

* * *

Motorway into Belfast. Reaching a phone booth ...derstown on the entrance into the city, he tapped ...e's phone number. It rang repeatedly but there was ...ly. He returned to his car and came to another ...kpoint. Again he told the R.U.C. he was there on ...siness and gave his address. He passed the taxi rank outside the Falls Road beside the Smithfield Market and looked across to the terraced houses, packed close with satellite dishes and chimney pots that coughed out smoke.

He looked out to the Divis flats and the British army helicopter coming to land on top of them and the huge Tricolour painted down over the concrete. The tension was palpable. A patrol passed him, two soldiers back to back and a third behind, nervous, their guns downwards at an angle. As he drove down the Falls Road he passed the Royal Victoria Hospital and felt something inside him but disregarded it. Further up the road, he looked up at the murals on the end walls, pictures of hooded paramilitaries and anger.

Wire cages and cameras.

It appeared to him that it was all hopeless, that Jenny, the troubles, Dublin, Belfast had an aura of inevitability about it. He had a picture in his mind of a difficult child screaming for love, its hands stretched out, pleading for love.

He was stopped again by a patrol, they had been watching him and searched his car. After further questions he was told to get out of the area. He went to another phone booth covered in graffiti. Beside it, the pavement was painted with continuous green, white and orange. He made a second call to Valerie, she answered and they arranged to meet in the city centre.

He was stopped once more and questioned. He drove to a car-park behind the Hipark Shopping Centre and walked the Golden Mile to Lower Donegal Street where he sat in a coffee shop and watched men put up lines of Christmas lights. He drank coffee and read about the slaughter of the soldiers.

Valerie came in wearing blue jeans, a grey jumper and doc martins, her dark hair cut tight. She came around, sat and looked into his face, her eyes curious and anxious. She asked him about his injury. He told her briefly about the men coming to the night-club, but without detail.

'Where's Jenny?' he asked.

'I don't know. They've put her in some hospital, I don't know, but she's alive and she's come out of it, they're blaming me you know, her sister rang, screaming at me that I was a traitor, all that shit.'

'Her sister Rachel?'

'Yeah, she's so vindictive, she, I used to like her but since Jenny's been in Dublin she's really changed. I think Wallace has her in his pocket.'

Valerie took out a cigarette, lit it and really easy with it asked: 'Are you all right? I mean can you walk ... look Brian ... I'm sorry for ringing you at home.'

She sucked on her cigarette and continued:

'She ... I think there was a bad row because she wouldn't leave my place, she'd bruises all over her arms, she had nowhere to go, I told her to stay with me in Belfast.'

'Where is she?' he asked.

'I swear I don't know.'

'Valerie! Which hospital?'

'I swear, it's not that simple, she could be anywhere.'

There was a lengthy pause. Valerie dragged on her cigarette and tapped it into an ashtray.

'You know after the Abercorn bomb, Wallace went crazy...'

She paused and blew out smoke.

'He's a thug, nothin' more, that's all and I wouldn't be surprised if he's creamin' off money for himself, he's like that. He draws diagrams of tattoos all night. He won't talk to anyone, he just stares at the TV with the phone beside him, Jesus you should see his tattoos, they're disgustin', eerie!'

'I know. I had a special show, a midnight performance ... listen Valerie I don't want a biography, and I don't want a history lesson.'

'They call him the Bishop, I mean it's so ironic, him a Bishop. Jesus, it's sick.'

She squashed her cigarette into the ashtray.

'If I'm seen with you ...'

'Where is she?' he asked.

'You know Brian, they only let her go to Dublin on condition that she didn't get involved.'

'I asked you a question ... where is she?'

'That's the way they are Brian, that guy Wallace is mad into her mother, he'll do anything for her and I mean anything. After Jenny found that lump in her back, they sent her to the Belfast City Hospital for radiography. Wallace had the money. She told me her mother paid the bill ... in cash, I'm so worried for Jenny, I know her, I'm so afraid she won't pull through this one.'

'Listen Valerie you've got to ring the hospitals, you've got to find out which one she's in. Do this for me, will you? There aren't that many.'

She lit a cigarette, her hand shaking.

'I got such a fright when Jenny told me what happened, you're the only person I can talk to, she couldn't calm down, I couldn't calm her, for days she stared into the fire, she didn't know who I was. I told her only to take one to help and the next morning she takes my whole stash. I don't know who cut them, I think there's some bad shit around.'

He looked into Valerie's face.

'Listen Valerie, will you shut up, calm down, I don't want to hear any more of that shit, find out where she is. Jesus remember it was you who found her the last time.'

Valerie sniffled.

'I know the way you're looking at me, but it wasn't my

fault, honestly.'

'With drugs, Valerie it's always someone else's fault, isn't it.'

Valerie cried openly, flushing her guilt and her care out in front of him. He put his hand over and touched her shoulder.

'Listen you've got to tell me where Wallace and that bitch live.'

She stopped.

'You're not serious, you're not going over there, no way, Brian, are you mad?...you can't drive into the North and do that, Jesus, you can't go near Wallace. That man's afraid of nothing, he doesn't know fear.'

'Valerie, you must understand I can do this because it doesn't fuckin' matter to me ... it doesn't fucking matter anymore you understand', he shouted.

'Jesus Brian ... keep your voice down. Jesus please ... Brian please.'

She flicked her cigarette repeatedly and after a time she said in a low voice,'I know he goes to church on Sundays over there, can you believe it? I think he stays there at weekends, and goes to church, it makes me feel sick even to think of it'.

He pulled out the ordinance map.

'You can't spread that out in here.' Valerie said.

He was firm.

'Take this pen, mark the church, mark the fucking road, write down the address.' he ordered, and started to lay out the map over the square table.

'They live out in Dundonald, East Belfast, out past the Stormont buildings in an estate out there. Show me, turn it around.' she said.

She got a biro and tapped the paper.

'There, that's where they live, that's it.'

She marked the avenue.

'Write down the address' he demanded.

She did.

'Are you sure?'

'Sure? I'm sure, I've been there enough times.'

'Coffee?'

'No, more coffee, no, I can't be seen with you, please Brian.'

'Don't be crazy.'

'Brian ...'

She stared at him and stood up.

'You're in Belfast now, you don't see anything, you don't hear anything.' she whispered, 'You speak to no-one. I'll wait by my phone.'

He stared at her.

'Listen to me, don't leave that phone, do you hear?'

Valerie moved around the table and gave him a kiss.

'What's that for?'

'You take care,' she said and walked out of the coffee shop.

He wondered if the girl was setting him up. He wondered why he had shouted.

* * *

He went into a shop and changed punts into sterling. He took the escalator downstairs to a pay-phone. He found the yellow pages and rang around the hospitals.

He left and entered a pub in Upper Church Lane where he ate Champ and brown bread. After a time he rang Valerie, she'd found nothing, she couldn't understand it. He asked her if they might have put her in under a different name, she doubted it but asked him to ring later that evening. He spent the afternoon in the Strand Inn. That evening he rang and arranged to meet her. He ordered pints of Guinness and watched the whole ceremony, the way the man filled the glass three-quarters, the way he put the glass down on a damp cloth beside the taps and then over time the dark grey water turned solid black, the froth curled and settled into a clear line of cream and the barman returning, bending the glass under the pumps and pulling the tap. The ale pouring out as he straightened the glass.

He listened to two men talking beside him, they sounded like reporters. He drank time through and then Valerie entered, breathless.

She sat down, placed her hat on the counter and took off her headphones.

'Did you find her?' he asked.

'No'.

'Jesus Christ'.

'I don't know where she is ... I don't know anymore. I don't know where they've put her'.

There was a silence.

'What will you do if you find her?' she asked.

He put his two fingers to the bridge of his nose.

'I don't know, get her to Dublin, get her a place, what would you like?' he asked, watching her carefully.

'Bacardi and coke, thanks. No, get us a hot whiskey, I think I'm getting a cold,' she said 'You've no idea what that would mean to her, she really has nothing here, she's lost, does your wife?' she trailed away.

'What?'

'Nothing ... it's none of my business.'

The drink arrived. Valerie sipped a little and put the whiskey down. She had a clove in her mouth which she started to crunch, she looked hard at him.

'Why are you doing this?'

Brian waited and replied, 'She needs it ... someone's got to do something.'

'This is honour for you, that's it, most married men would walk away.'

He took some Guinness.

'I dunno, call it what you like.'

'This is an honour thing for you, that's what it is.'

She looked into his eyes and continued:

'Jesus, I didn't think there was honour anymore, I thought it was use, or be used, that people like you didn't exist, I mean you could have walked away from her. This is crazy.'

'I took her on with all her baggage and I don't want her to die.'

'You're stronger than I thought. Just don't end up dead.'

'Honour, is that what you call it?'

He smiled cynically. Time passed.

'You know in the beginnin',' she said, 'I didn't approve, you being married an' all, then I realised she was really happy with you, I've never seen her like that, no-one else has done that.'

'I know it's okay, I understand, don't go into it, Valerie.'

He supped on his pint and continued.

'That's not why I'm here, and I want you to know.' He leaned towards her. 'You must know it's finished.'

Valerie made a face as though she'd heard it before and said, 'I hadn't seen her for months ... I mean since she left Dublin ... listen I can't hang around here.'

She drank, pulled on her cigarette and said, 'she told me you made her laugh, that you had this old record player, is that true.'

'Yes, I'm afraid so.'

'I tell you, you were the only one who could handle her temper.'

'Valerie, this is over, I'm not messing my wife around anymore. This one's for Jenny but that's it, I mean it Valerie.

'She loves you, you know that.'

'Jesus you're like a nun with a flick-knife.'

Valerie made a face.

'That's good Brian, that's very good.'

She put her cap on.

He stood up and said.

'What you're doing is right, the best thing you've ever done, stay by that phone and try a different name when you're ringing the hospitals.'

... 'Okay?' he insisted.

'Okay.' she said putting on her headphones.

'Keep ringing around, I'll ring you tomorrow morning.' he said.

She walked out.

He felt re-assured the way Valerie seemed to care, he thought back to the bath and how good she'd been helping Jenny through the scar of her attempted suicide.

* * *

The next morning, Sunday. He took his breakfast from the landlady at the B&B, paid his bill and drove out to Dundonald, past Stormont and its lanterned driveway. As he neared the housing estate he saw the church to the right behind some trees. He took the car to the entrance with its imposing black gates. There was a notice-board set into the ground, inscribed into it the gold letters:

Church of Ireland.
Sunday service.
8.30 a.m. Holy Communion.
11.00 a.m. Morning Service.
7.00 p.m. Evening Service.

He looked at his watch, it was ten o'clock. He drove the car around and brought it into the housing estate, a simple estate with well manicured lawns, clean fences and an air of tidiness. The house was in a cul-de-sac on the corner. He slowed and noticed two men in a parked car. One of them sat up, he accelerated and drove past. He turned the car at the top of the road and drove back feigning disinterest.

He tried to sing with the music but it came out nervous. He drove onto the main avenue down to the bottom and made a left by the church, pulled up, waited and watched. Before the hour, people dressed neat and subdued, walked in, some with prayer books, others with children.

A Granada parked, Wallace got out, his thick frame, his face full of wariness, and walked Jenny's mother and her sister across the road and into the church. Brian waited and watched. After some time he left the car and approached the church. The congregation sang out loud with strength and commitment:

> *'Through the night of doubt and sorrow,*
> *Onward goes the pilgrim band,*
> *Singing songs of expectation,*
> *Marching to the promised land.'*

He listened, waiting a while before going to a side door of the church. The rector read:

> *'All mine enemies whisper together against me.*
> *Even against me do they imagine this evil.*
> *An evil disease say they cleaveth fast unto him and now that he lieth he shall rise up no more.*
> *Yea, even mine own familiar friend, whom I trusted, who did also eat of my bread, hath laid great wait for me.'*

From where he stood in the side chapel, he watched Wallace seated in his pew, resolute in hypocritical sanctity but as he watched, his breathing increased and a fierce rage boiled up in him, a rage that fermented revenge, then as if seized in a trance, he began to make his way down through the middle of the church. The congregation stared at him.

He shouted. 'Wallace, where have you put her, where is she, where's Jenny?'

The rector stopped reading. Brian neared the back of the church, at the last minute, Wallace recognised him.

'I don't fuckin' believe it!' he exclaimed.

Brian came at him, his crutch raised. Wallace stood up out of his seat. Brian lifted the crutch over his shoulders and swung it wildly, hitting Wallace square on the face, breaking open his nose and lips. The man fell to the ground and Brian went in with his fists hitting Wallace time and again until the man was covered in blood.

Jenny's mother screamed. Rachel's mouth wide open. The congregation stared in dismay and retreated.

'Please everyone, please! In the name of God!' the rector shouted.

Rachel began to scream. Brian stood up, in his hands the bloody crutch.

People afraid of this madness stared at him, aghast. He pointed the crutch at Wallace's bloody face and ran out.

The organist upstairs played 'Onward Christian Soldiers'. The song sheets and prayer books were speckled with fresh blood.

* * *

When he rang Valerie, she told him that she had found her under Wallace's name in the Royal Victoria Hospital. She shouted it out to him again and again. He slammed the phone back on its hook and drove his car at speed to the River Lagan and the Victoria Hospital. He knew he had done something terribly wrong, in their church. He blessed himself.

* * *

He ran into the ward. Jenny looked at him not recognising him at first. He came in close.

'Brian, oh Brian!' she exclaimed and put her arms out surprised and happy.

'Jenny, c'mon get out, we're going.'

She wrapped her arms around him. He pulled back the bedclothes.

'We're goin', we're goin', where are we goin'?' she asked.

She was slow. She didn't understand but she wouldn't let him go. He pulled back her bedclothes.

'C'mon Jenny, trust me.'

She stared bewildered.

'I knew ye'd come , I knew it, I knew it.'
'Quick, be quick, get up.'
She held him tight around his waist.
'Jenny, quick.'
'I must get my clothes.'
'Forget it, we haven't time, you'll have to make it to the lift, c'mon.'

He put his arms under her and lifted her out of the bed, leaning on his crutch.

'Oh Brian, I can't.' she wailed.
'Yes, you can Jenny, courage, Jenny remember courage, look into my eyes.'

He counted to ten.

'Put on your slippers, easy, easy.'

The other patients in the ward stared at him, curious and tired. The slippers were on. He lifted her arms around his shoulders.

The beat.

They walked down the corridor towards the lifts. When they reached the end of the passage-way, they heard shouting.

'Excuse me, excuse me, excuse me, Miss Wallace, Miss Wallace?'

He pressed the button for the lift but the lights remained unchanged. They opened the glass door leading onto the staircase and ran down. As they reached the turn, the lift doors opened. Wallace stepped into the passageway, sweaty, burning with anger, his face covered in dried blood. He didn't see them. He made his way hurriedly towards her ward.

A nurse ran to the stairway area, stopped for a moment and turned back. Wallace cursed and closed his bulky jacket as though concealing a weapon but through the glass he saw his prey. Brian lifted his crutch and jammed it across the handles of the stairway doors. Wallace pointed at him, his two fingers together and shouted, 'Yer dead ye bastard, dead!'

Brian took her onto the first landing and they went down two flights, nurses and an intern chasing after them. When they reached the ground floor they turned back into a corridor and ran to the end of a passageway, avoiding patients and doctors. They found a second staircase and started going down even further, eventually arriving at an underground passageway which ran under the entire building.

He turned around. Two security men and nurses chased. One of the nurses screamed, 'She's one of our patients.'

Wallace was directly behind them, his eyes bulging.

'We can't, I'll never make it, I'll never make it.' Jenny called out.

They reached a turn on the corridor, made a left and moved into a second, smaller corridor and made towards a line of doors. There was a laundry basket, he pushed it aside and put his hand on the round metal door-handle. The door opened, he pulled Jenny in and closed it tight behind them.

It was dark, both of them gasped for breath. The room was cold. They waited and heard doors open and close. In the shadows he made out a shape.

'Quick.' he pleaded.

He grabbed her. They hid behind a tall metal cabinet. The room smelt of disinfectant.

Suddenly at that moment, the door swung open. The lights were switched on. It was the mortuary. On five tables in front of them lay the remains of men, labelled. One headless, its mutilated head resting beside it, another had no legs, a third disfigured by shrapnel, its torso ripped open.

He clasped his hand over her mouth. One of the security men swore and the door closed, the light remained on. They both stood transfixed in horror at the victims of violence.

'They're soldiers.' he said 'that land mine last week, Jesus Christ!'

Kissing the Orange

Jenny's eyes contorted in disbelief, she doubled up but nothing came.

'Close your eyes', he said, 'we're going, they'll be looking for my car, come on.'

She touched one of the bodies.

'What are you doing? What are you doing?' he asked.

She turned around with water in her eyes.

'Oh Brian.'

He opened the door slightly, listened and grabbed her.

'C'mon, let's move .... now.'

He pulled her behind him as they cut into another corridor, running for about thirty yards until they made their way up a small staircase. There was a handrail which she held tightly, they reached the top. 'Faster, faster,' he pleaded.

'No, no, I can't, I can't .'

'We're nearly there, we're nearly there, c'mon Jenny we've got to get out of here.'

Again they were on the ground floor of the hospital, two nurses walked towards them, unaware. They made their way towards the main entrance of the hospital but he looked down the never-ending corridor and saw security men running towards him, alarm in their faces.

'Stay as ye are, stay as ye are.' they shouted.

He pulled her back and turned into a corridor, through the staff restaurant. She crashed into a girl carrying a tray of plastic cups, steaming coffee splashed over the nurses heads.

'Stop, get those two, stop them.' someone shouted.

They ran towards the till and around the cashier on the stool, into the kitchen where chefs prepared food, their backs to these fugitives.

'Move it.' Brian screamed at her.

She hit into a stainless-steel shelving unit, saucepans fell to the ground, chefs turned surprised.

Suddenly they were out into the open, out into a yard and they ran between bins and vans into the car park. A hundred yards behind them, three men followed.

Wallace came around the side of the hospital. They moved between parked cars out towards perimeter walls, until they reached his car. Wallace ran towards them, waving his arms and shouting. Brian jumped into the car, opened her door and screamed: 'Jesus, Jenny, hurry up, get in, quick.'

He turned the engine over and slammed his door shut, the wheels spinning in acceleration. Wallace ran beside the car, a gun drawn. Brian got her head and pushed it down into her knees. The tyres screeched. There was no gunfire.

He took his car down the Falls Road past Beechmount, Whiterock, the Milltown Cemetery on his left, the Sinn Fein club on his right, the Anderstown Police Station splitting the road, Kennedy Way and onto the perimeter road. Wallace followed in his Granada. He overtook three, four, five cars, and on the inside another two cars waiting for a traffic light to change.

She turned and stared through the back window.

'Jesus slow down,' she pleaded.

She looked into his face as though deciding for that last time whether she was committed to this man or not and pointed frantically, screaming: 'Turn left here, here, here!' and then she said it, 'I love ye.'

'I hate your guts,' he replied.

'I love ye.'

'I hate your guts,' he repeated.

They went out on to the perimeter road, their eyes like one joined in a communion of adrenaline. Both of them repeating their prayer louder and louder. He was doing ninety, a hundred, a hundred and ten, passing out cars on the inner and outer lanes, all the time the two of them shouting –

'I love ye.'

'I hate your guts.'

'I love ye.'

'I hate your guts.'

'I love ye.'

'I hate your guts.'

He rounded a corner to see a line of cars in front of them, soldiers at the side and the caps of the RUC, two grey Landrovers covered in wire.

The words of his wife Ciara in his head: 'Brian, you can't beat the system, in the end the system will always get you.'

He increased speed, going in against the oncoming traffic on the right-hand side of the road, his lights full, his horn blaring and as he reached the checkpoint he braked. Two uniformed men ran towards him but instead of stopping he accelerated through them. One of the RUC officers jumped out of the way, a second man pulled out a revolver, smashing the butt of it against the windscreen. There were four, maybe five other men in green jackets and bullet-proof vests. They scattered.

He made it around a corner away from them, passing out cars, driving hard for about eight miles through to Glenavy, Jenny staring at him like she knew, she knew she'd got him all over again. Repeating their prayer over and over. The beat had returned, she was so sure of it.

Before Ballydonaghy he rounded a corner and slammed on the brakes, the car skidded to a halt. He put it into gear and swung in left through a wooded laneway and looked behind him, recognising the front of Wallace's car coming at him.

'Jesus Christ!' he said. 'He's still behind us, where are we?'

She didn't reply.

He drove through the wooded lane until he reached an intersection and a small bridge. Suddenly the car lifted off the ground and when it landed he lost control, skidding into a tree, leaving the left wing scrunched up. The engine stalled. He tried in desperation to restart it, turning it over and over. It was flooded. Ahead was an old farmhouse, walled in with broken stones, thick hedge growth, a hayshed and some outhouses.

He jumped out, grabbed her and ran through the buildings, towards the river which wound through this land, behind him Wallace roaring out his threats, his eyes bulging their violence. They ran through yellow gorse, climbed over a stone wall to the river's edge, her nightdress torn to shreds by brambles and gorse. They ran beside the river, looking for cover. Wallace gained. She was winded and exhausted. They were going nowhere. He looked across the river and it looked still and calm. In front of him there was a quagmire of reeds and long grass. He began to wade into the water. Wallace remained on the riverbank roaring obscenities and threats.

They got out ten, maybe, fifteen yards into the icy water, her grip loosened and the current pulled her away from him.

'No Jenny, no!' he shouted.

Her head went under, her eyes longing and resigned, accepting a hopeless destiny, wrapped in water and death. Her hair disappeared from his view. He kicked hard into the water and went down after her.

Time passed and the beat could be heard over that river.

He surfaced, opened his mouth and dived down again into the current, more time passed. No Brian. No Jenny. Every second a lifetime, every second, a second closer to death. As he descended, in his mind came the pictures of it all, the hospital, the violence in the church, his wife's crying eyes, his prayers in the sanctity of the monastery, his beautiful children reaching out for him, the goldfish, Jenny's temper, her wigs, the tears and the passion in her eyes, Ciara's words, 'I trust you so much I don't ever want to lose you!', the monk's words, 'A man must confront the thing he's most afraid of,' and then it all got deep and dark.

His search for her in the water was a search to inspire valour, to prove love, to tame insanity, to tempt death, to inspire strength.

A search for his own courage.

* * *

Wallace scanned the surface of the water but all was silent.

The top of the water broke and Brian's head appeared, his left arm around her neck swimming backwards, pulling her body towards the riverbank.

He reached the far ground, gasping for air, dragged her body up and turned it over, putting his arms around her waist, squeezing her stomach until water gushed out. He breathed deeply turned her over and put his mouth over hers, repeating this time and time again, pushing his life into her.

She began to cough, he rolled her on her side and squeezed in her rib cage. She vomited up water. He punched the air.

'Yes!' he cried triumphantly.

He leaned over her and repeated, 'Yes, yes, thank you Jenny, thank you.'

He stared into her face. Her eyes opened and she whispered, 'Don't thank me.'

She coughed again and forced a smile, 'Thank God, ye met me.'

He shook his head, his body supporting his arms, his face hanging over hers, water dripping down. She touched his mouth, running her finger over his lips and said with her eyes:

'Kiss me!'

He smiled and said:

'Kiss you ... I'll kiss the Orange in you.'

'Ye know I love ye, I've always loved ye,' she said.

He bent down and kissed her twice.

'Well Jenny, I hate your guts.'

And repeated:

'I hate your guts!'

She smiled weakly and closed her eyes. He looked into the face, the face he would always wish to look into, her slight eyebrows, her thin nose, her skin shrivelled and white as alabaster.

He turned his head to Wallace standing on the far side of the riverbank, his gun levelled at Brian's head, and shouted:

'It's over Wallace, it's over leave it, throw it away.'

Slowly Wallace began to squeeze on the trigger but he hesitated and dropped his arm to his side.

Brian turned his eyes back towards her and said:

'Jenny, I've got to buy a ring for someone.'

She said, 'I know, Brian, I know, ye know, ye buy her a ring, the biggest ring, the biggest ring of all.'

'I will Jenny, I will.' he whispered.

She said 'Exactly.'

She said 'Exactly.'

She said 'Exactly.'

And she decided then that a single moment would give a life, a future, a world, a child and that that moment would be with someone ... with someone else.

That evening the clouds broke up and the evening light penetrated through, a slow warm light casting its luminous veil across the sky, full of saffron and yellow. A light that bathed a troubled Ireland in its history and its destiny, a light that brought with it a new hope, a new reunion and a clean love that would finally deny the pallor of rain.

* * *

'Ciara will you dance?'
'Only if it's the same Brian ... the same as before.'
'I'll get the gramaphone.'
'I've forgotten the steps ... we'll have to start all over ... you're thinking ... what are you thinking?'
'Nothing ... I've grown up ... that's all.'
'Thanks for the ring ... an emerald, it's perfect ... perfect.'
'Then Ciara let's dance ... dance ... dance.'

THE END